Mobile
business strategies

Mobile
business strategies

Understanding the technologies and opportunities

Jouni Paavilainen

 Addison-Wesley in partnership with IT Press

An imprint of **Pearson Education**

London / Boston / Indianapolis / New York / Mexico City / Toronto / Sydney / Tokyo / Singapore / Hong Kong / Cape Town / New Delhi / Madrid / Paris / Amsterdam / Munich / Milan / Stockholm

PEARSON EDUCATION LIMITED

Head Office:
Edinburgh Gate
Harlow CM20 2JE
Tel: +44 (0)1279 623623
Fax: +44 (0)1279 431059

London Office:
128 Long Acre, London WC2E 9AN
Tel: +44 (0)20 7447 2000
Fax: +44 (0)20 7240 5771
Website:www.aw.com/cseng/

First published in Great Britain in 2002

© IT Press 2001

The right of Jouni Paavilainen to be identified as author
of this work has been asserted by him in accordance
with the Copyright, Designs and Patents Act 1988.

ISBN 0 201 78898 5

British Library Cataloguing in Publication Data
A CIP catalogue record for this book can be obtained from the British Library.
Library of Congress Cataloging in Publication Data. Applied for.

10 9 8 7 6 5 4 3 2 1

Designed by Sue Lamble
Typeset by Pantek Arts Ltd, Maidstone, Kent.
Printed and bound in Great Britain by Biddles Ltd of Guildford and King's Lynn.

The Publishers' policy is to use paper manufactured from sustainable forests.

Contents

1   Introduction to the mobile internet   1

Contents

5   Location-based services – potential for operators and partners   152

6   Portals – a single plate for various dishes   179

Contents

Index of case studies

About the author

Jouni Paavilainen works for Accenture Digital Innovation Centre, in Finland. He is currently responsible for mobile commerce business models and strategies within the centre where his role is to bridge modern technologies to successful m-commerce applications with business potential.

Mobile Business Strategies is the second book by Jouni Paavilainen. He is also the author of *Doing Business Over the Internet* published in 1999.

For further information, please contact: jouni.paavilainen@accenture.com

Preface

Mobile phones are no longer just a means of calling another person. In several countries, mobile devices are used to pay for merchandise, receive time sensitive information and send e-mail messages. Additionally, corporations use mobile phones to access critical business information and send tasks to field workers, regardless of time or location.

In recent years, several global mega-trends have started to emerge, creating exciting business opportunities and concepts. Widespread usage of credit cards, the phenomenal explosion of the internet and rising mobile phone penetration have paved the way for advanced mobile applications that enable both consumers and corporations to access personalized services. Therefore, mobile devices are becoming an important part of the lives of ordinary people. Using a mobile phone, they can buy a soft drink when passing a vending machine, receive e-mails immediately after they are sent, order a taxi without knowing their current location and get notified if they forgot to pay the electricity bill.

Ubiquity, intimacy, time sensitivity and location awareness are key concepts that make mobile business so different from 'traditional' e-commerce. Business professionals can no longer wait until colleagues have time to replicate their e-mails. Instead, for urgent matters, they send an instant message or push e-mail. Travellers can use location-based hotel finders to find their way in strange cities. Consumers subscribe to instant stock quote services, pushed into their mobile phones, to keep up with the stock market. Ordinary people install credit and payment cards into their mobile phones to be able to buy online, regardless of their location. Without doubt, the mobile revolution offers interesting business opportunities to everybody. At the same time, it transforms existing business structures and poses threats to traditional players, especially those in the fields of telecommunications and finance.

This book takes a look at emerging mobile trends. In addition, it discusses the roles of financial institutions, operators, content providers and other parties engaged in the mobile commerce value chain. The basic issues of technology are covered from a strategic viewpoint and the reader becomes familiarized with the possibilities and limitations of the mobile environment. As possible applications are introduced, both consumer and corporate user segments are discussed in detail. Additionally, the book covers location-based services and identifies possible target segments for various location-dependent applications. Finally, mobile portal strategies are reviewed and individual recommendations are given to web portals, content providers, mobile operators, financial institutions, system integrators and application developers.

For additional information, updates and discussion, visit:

www.mobilecommercestrategy.com

Acknowledgements

Writing a book is always a back-breaking, tough process that requires a lot, especially from loved ones. Therefore, I would like to express my deepest gratitude to Jonna, my wife, who has patiently been there for me. Jonna did not provide only emotional help. She also provided her guidance regarding graphics and other issues. Thank you for being supportive.

Hall and Judy Burford have left their fingerprints on this book. Almost ten years ago, they hosted my exchange student year in the USA. Judy provided her special guidance in writing this book and helped me to correct some of the mistakes in my English grammar. Hall and Judy, you are very special to me. Thank you for your caring during these years.

I have the privilege of working with the world's best teams and individual experts in the mobile commerce arena. Accenture's Mobile Internet Center of Excellence in Helsinki has provided me with guidance and support during the writing process. Several specialists have reviewed this book before it was published. I would like to give special thanks to Janne Lautanala, Mika Saastamoinen and Paula Verho from the Helsinki Mobile Center who all took time to comment on this book. Markku Silèn, Juho Malmberg, Kaarlo Hirvi and Mikko Hirvonen have also supported me before and during the writing process. In addition, Pasi Pentikäinen and Yacine Zaitri have given me a lot. Their knowledge and expertise have helped me a great deal in understanding the technical requirements of mobile world.

I would also like to mention the following people who gave their emotional support or facilitated my writing in one form or the other:

Juha Paavilainen
Martti and Marja Taimela
Tatu Räisänen
Kimmo Aaltonen
Matti Alava
Ari Sahanen
Jukka Riivari

Peppe Mancuso
Mikko Laurila

Any opinions expressed in this book are solely those of the author and should not be taken as an endorsement by Accenture.

1

Introduction to the mobile internet

The definition of mobile business

This book defines mobile business as:

"The exchange of goods, services and information using mobile technology."

Mobile business is a broad definition that includes communication, transactions and different value added services, which are made available using mobile terminals such as phones, PDAs and pagers. Today, most of the attention is around consumer services but business-to-business and business-to-employee segments are also important. The term "mobile internet" has been introduced to emphasize the synergy between internet applications and the mobile world. In this book, the mobile internet is defined as:

"internet access from a mobile device, such as a phone, a PDA (Personal Digital Assistant), a car information system, a watch, a two-way pager or some other device capable of accessing the internet regardless of time or location."

Another essential definition for this book is mobile commerce. This is referred to as "transactions with monetary value, conducted using the mobile internet". This definition covers business-to-business, business-to-consumer and consumer-to-consumer transactions. Traditional voice calls are not included in the definition of mobile commerce, but services using voice recognition in order to enable commercial transactions fall into this category. Mobile commerce is a sub-set of electronic commerce in terms of technical issues. However, the term "mobile e-commerce" is a bit misleading because the business models and value chain are totally different from electronic commerce. Additionally, mobile commerce is not a truncated form of e-commerce but a new, innovative way of conducting time-critical transactions regardless of location.

Main elements and investment opportunities

Mobile internet can be divided into three main elements, presenting a horizontal approach to the core applications. The elements are communication, commerce and value added services. By introducing vertical target groups, corporate and consumer, most mobile internet applications can be broadly categorized (Table 1.1).

TABLE 1.1 ■ The three main elements of the mobile internet

	Corporate	Consumer
Communication	■ Voice ■ E-mail ■ Instant messaging ■ Unified messaging ■ Team working tools ■ Videotelephony	■ Voice ■ E-mail ■ Instant messaging ■ Unified messaging ■ Chat ■ Videotelephony ■ Community services ■ Digital postcards
Commerce	■ Retail ■ Location-based commerce ■ Stock broking ■ Banking ■ Corporate auctions ■ Multichannel commerce ■ Insurance ■ Reservations ■ Advertising	■ Retail ■ Location-based commerce ■ Comparison shopping inside the store ■ Ticketing ■ Stock broking ■ Banking ■ Auctions ■ Multichannel commerce ■ Music ■ Gambling and betting ■ Ringing tones and phone icons ■ Insurance ■ Reservations ■ Advertising

	Corporate	Consumer
Value added services	■ Industry and financial news ■ Customer relationship management ■ Management reporting ■ Fleet management ■ Sales force automation ■ Employee self service ■ Travel management ■ Recruitment ■ Supply chain management ■ Human resources management ■ Security ■ Remote control	■ News ■ Entertainment ■ Travel ■ Driving directions ■ Location-based services ■ Security ■ Domestic remote control ■ Calendar ■ Society services ■ Instant message services

The applications of mobile internet are generated from four different sources:

1. Fixed internet applications, such as e-mail, news and stock broking. The form factor of a mobile device is taken into consideration when developing the services. However, applications are based on the fixed internet. Therefore, the time to market is considerably shortened. Another way to generate mobile applications is to design mobile extensions for existing internet solutions. These extensions are not available when using the service with a PC. Instant messaging used with online auctions falls into this category.

2. Content-driven multichannel services. TV, radio or print is used in conjunction with mobile phones. The new channel is used in order to generate transactions, increase interactivity or provide secure and instant payment channels to consumers.

3. Corporate systems. Real-time information from the corporate legacy systems is used in order to generate mobile applications. For example, management reporting, sales force automation and employee self service is used to increase efficiency and cut down costs.

4. Technology-enabled applications. Instant messaging, location technologies and personalization are used to innovate new services which are able to push time and location critical content to mobile devices. These applications are personalized for the user. This category has enormous untapped potential because it is something completely new. It uses the characteristics of a mobile device creatively.

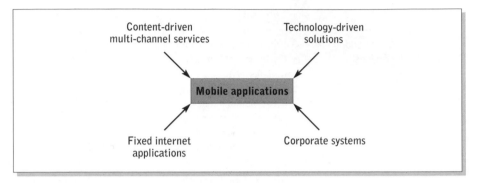

FIGURE 1.1 ■ Mobile applications are generated from four different sources

The players in the mobile internet arena focus on applications most suitable for their interests and business strategy. Internet and mobile phone penetration, together with the user patterns and behavior in various countries, define the most appropriate approach. Countries with high mobile phone and internet penetration may be suitable targets for services integrating the two into a value added service. Fixed portals can offer PC interface for easy set-up and personalization of a mobile portal. This way, the small screen and character input limitations may be overcome because most of the customers also have a fixed internet connection. On the other hand, countries with low internet penetration are a target for companies developing independent mobile applications. For example, location-sensitive driving directions, mobile e-mail, ticketing and stock broking are all applications that do not necessarily need a fixed internet connection to overcome the inadequacies of mobile terminals. Finally, some countries with very low mobile phone and internet penetration may be immature markets for the deployment of mobile services. Most developing countries are still in a state where investments in mobile internet technology cannot be justified.

There are numerous promising investment opportunities in the mobile internet arena. Companies specializing in location and personalization technology have the potential to become very successful. Most mobile operators are looking for increased revenue from data services as the profit margin from voice services is dropping. Location-based services address one of the core characteristics of mobile phones by enabling innovative services ranging from position-sensitive advertising to driving directions. Therefore, mobile operators consider the deployment of location technology when upgrading their networks for future terminals.

However, only a few companies specialize in the development of location-sensitive applications. Their importance is likely to increase as venture capitalists see emerging possibilities in applications enabled by location technology.

Another promising technology is instant messaging. Time sensitive and location-independent applications bring another dimension to the information provided by fixed internet services. Would you like to know when the stock in which you invested last week falls 25%? How about some notice when the balance of your bank account is in danger of being zero? You could even allow the electric company to send the bill directly to your mobile device, making it payable while sitting in a train. Imagine the increase in customer service, not to mention the cost savings, that companies are able to generate by introducing these services in markets with high mobile phone penetration. All of the above services use instant messaging that can be pushed to a mobile terminal in real time.

Most of the companies moving into mobile internet use their core competencies to market services and products faster. Systems integrators offer mobile extensions for legacy systems they have implemented. This way, they are able to move into new fields of business quickly while existing customer relationships are retained. Most systems integrators offer value added services to corporations integrating mobile channels into customer relationship management, enterprise resource planning and supply chain management. Additionally, content providers use their core competencies in order to offer mobile information services. For example, sports channels create mobile extensions for their existing programs, enabling viewers to be updated when they are away from their TV. News channels, such as CNN, have already taken an aggressive approach towards mobility by launching WAP sites in cooperation with partners who range from operators to device manufacturers. Mobile operators are also exploiting their core competencies in order to create portal sites using the latest features, such as location and micro-payment processing.

Corporations may choose to specialize in a certain technology for strategic reasons. Mobile operators offering portal services may want to introduce mobile e-mail and chat in order to increase customer loyalty. They may also offer financial services to support mobile commerce. In doing so, mobile operators could remove banks from the mobile commerce value chain by providing the same services without the burden of expensive "brick and mortar" premises. In addition, systems integrators and application developers acquire expertise in location and personalization technologies to be better equipped for the new wave of mobile applications. This way, they can move ahead of their competitors and gain a competitive edge in the markets.

Important technologies and innovations

WAP and XHTML

WAP (Wireless Application Protocol) is an industry standard for mobile internet applications. Application developers around the world use WAP to create solutions for mobile data and communication. An open standard, it has been developed in cooperation with numerous companies from various segments of the mobile industry. Mobile operators, device manufacturers, software developers and many others have been involved in WAP Forum, the industry consortium dedicated to bringing information services to mobile devices. WAP

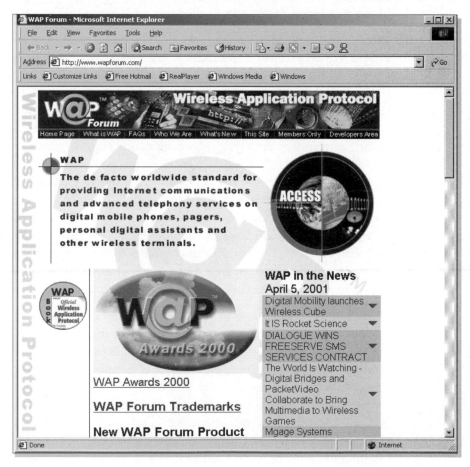

FIGURE 1.2 ■ The website of WAP Forum

Forum was initially launched in 1997 by Nokia, Ericsson, Motorola and Phone.com (recently renamed Openwave). Since its inception, WAP forum has been responsible for wireless protocol specification and its contribution to several industry groups and standard bodies. The organization has expanded rapidly and acquired strong industry backing from companies such as Microsoft, Deutsche Telecom, France Telecom and 3Com.

WAP Forum was founded primarily to integrate the two booming markets: Telecom and the internet. Since the introduction of WAP, the two markets have been able to reach synergic advantages by combining their strengths and driving development in a desirable direction. Open internet standards have already paved the way for WAP. Now the limitations of mobile devices will be taken into consideration with the emergence of WAP services. A fixed internet connection and the mobile internet are very different. Mobile devices have substantially smaller screens and keypads than PCs. Additionally, power consumption, small

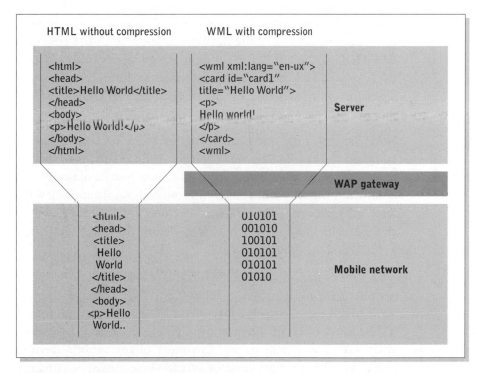

FIGURE 1.3 ■ Traditional big pipe small pipe problem. WML is compressed by the WAP gateway before transportation to mobile network. WAP browser of a mobile phone is able to convert compressed tags back to original form

memory and less powerful CPUs restrict the use of mobile devices for the "surfing" we experience with the fixed internet today. Mobile data networks are different as well. They have less bandwidth and connection stability than the fixed networks. In addition, the availability of the network connection cannot be guaranteed at all times. This is also the case with the introduction of new mobile networks – because they cannot instantly cover all the land areas, they are only available in the biggest cities. For all of these reasons, platform and bearer independent Wireless Application Protocol was developed. Wireless Markup Language, WML, is used to define the graphical layout of the service. WML is optimized for small screens and various input devices. Because the bandwidth is limited in mobile networks, WML is compressed by the WAP Gateway before transportation to a mobile device. This way, the speed can be enhanced while the load on mobile networks is decreased.

The use of WAP services is slow and cumbersome with circuit-switched networks. The initial connection takes a long time and there is a data call charge for browsing the services. This makes circuit-switched WAP expensive compared to the next generation of packet-switched networks, where the customer is charged according to the data transmitted. With the new GPRS (Europe) and 1XRTT (North America) networks, connection is always on, enabling push e-mail and an instant connection to numerous innovative services. Therefore, it is likely that the use of WAP services will explode with the introduction of the new, packet-switched networks.

WAP has raised the question of whether there is a need for a completely new standard for mobile data provisioning. Additionally, there have been debates that WAP will be short-lived because the new mobile networks with substantial bandwidth capacity will soon be introduced. Application developers and systems integrators have also pointed out that it will be very expensive to design two netcentric applications that generate the same information; one for HTML and the other for WML

The next evolution of WAP (WAP 2.0) is being developed to overcome the problems inherent in WAP technology. WAP 2.0 uses the basic profile of XHTML Basic (eXtensible HyperText Markup Language) to replace WML in a Wireless Application Environment. XHTML Basic is backwards compatible with WAP and it will be used in most of the mobile devices from 2002 onwards. The ultimate goal of XHTML technology is to create a single markup language for both mobile and fixed internet worlds.

Several industry leaders have joined to support XHTML standard. Mobile phone manufacturers (Nokia, Ericsson, Motorola, Siemens), Operators (Vodafone, Orange, T-Mobil, Sonera) and many others (Accenture, Adobe, Sun Microsystems, AOL, CNN) have expressed their commitment to the new markup language. Therefore, it seems that XHTML is likely to succeed in its mission to become a de facto standard of mobile and fixed internet.

XHTML is not the only improvement in the WAP 2.0 standard. The WAP protocol stack introduced in the WAP 1.0 standard has been extended to support common internet standards, such as TCP/IP and HTTP. For application developers, this is a major improvement, because communication between a WAP 2.0 compatible client and the origin server can be conducted using HTTP. The first version of WAP required a WAP proxy server between the client and the origin server. With WAP 2.0, this is no longer a necessity. However, WAP proxy servers may be used to optimize the communication process and to provide advanced features, such as push functionality, location awareness and privacy.

Push WAP is one of the most exciting features of the WAP 2.0 specification. It extends hugely popular SMS messaging and offers an easy interface for receiving real-time alerts and notifications. When the user receives a push message, the WAP browser is automatically started. The user can follow links in the message and download additional information easily. Real-time e-mail notifications, auction alerts and mobile chat are just some of the services suited to Push WAP.

Security has been one of the major concerns in the first version of WAP. The WAP proxy server was the vulnerable link, preventing end-to-end security. This was caused by a blind moment in the encoding/decoding process when data was not encrypted properly. Banks and other financial institutions solved the problem by placing the WAP proxy within company premises, which was the only way to properly secure the communication. With WAP 2.0, enhanced security can be attained by using the wireless profiles of common internet protocols: Transport Layer Security, HTTP and TCP. This way, data is transferred between the client and the server securely without blind moments in the proxy server.

WAP 2.0 introduces the User Agent Profile (UAProf), a service that provides a mechanism for describing phone capabilities and user preferences to an application server. With UAProf, application developers can design solutions that take phone and user characteristics into consideration. Because of variable screen sizes, input methods and data capabilities, UAProf is an essential feature in WAP 2.0.

Application developers must adapt quickly to the changing market situation. When developing mass market applications, they have to consider WAP and XHTML phone penetration among the target group. It takes some time before the penetration of XHTML is high enough for application development. The phenomenon is similar to the web, where application developers have to consider browser capabilities before introducing new services. In the beginning, frames could not be used because most people had web browsers which did not support them. Later, some multimedia effects were impossible because they required plug-ins installed in only a small percentage of the web browsers. The same pattern continues with mobile technologies and, therefore, application developers need to build services which are accessible to as many users as possible.

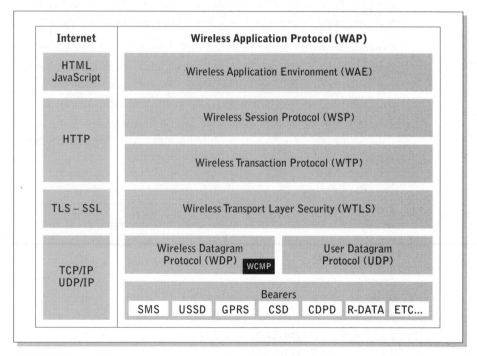

FIGURE 1.4 ■ WAP and internet standards in comparison   Source: WAP Forum

One of the most common misconceptions about WAP is that the gateway and applications are controlled by the mobile operator. On the contrary, WAP applications can be developed and managed by individual companies which have their own gateway and security components. For example, a company with Lotus Notes-based e-mail is able to offer WAP e-mail by attaching a special software component to Lotus Notes. This way, employees connect directly to a corporate Remote Access Server (RAS) to retrieve their e-mails. Information with a low or medium security rating does not require additional encryption procedures because the Notes and the WAP server reside inside the firewall. A company with its own WAP server has complete control over the information and applications transferred to a mobile device. This way, the applications can be used regardless of the user's mobile operator. Therefore, companies using multiple operators are able to deploy corporate WAP applications that are accessible to everyone.

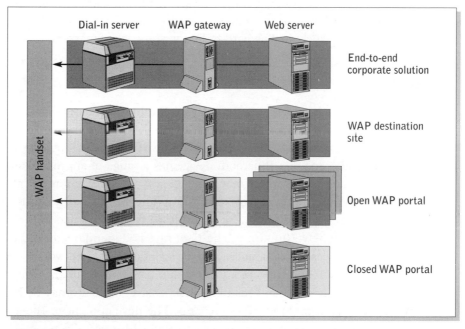

FIGURE 1.5 ■ The four deployment options of WAP in a circuit-switched network. End-to-end corporate solution uses internal WAP gateway for increased security. WAP destination site has an external dial-in server, but uses its own WAP gateway and web server. Open WAP portal allows users to access a dial-in server and WAP gateway for external internet browsing. Closed WAP portal has taken a "walled garden" approach

Strategic decisions regarding WAP deployment are based on two fundamental factors: timing and partners. The penetration of internet-capable mobile devices and the type of service define the right market entry conditions. Markets with high WAP device penetration are suited for horizontal, mass market consumer services. In contrast, vertical WAP services, like corporate e-mail and team working tools, can be deployed as soon as all the employees have appropriate terminals in hand. In both horizontal and vertical markets, early entry is more expensive because of high infrastructure and development costs.

However, early entry helps a company acquire competitive advantage over its competitors and prepares the organization to adopt the new technology. Another fundamental factor regarding WAP deployment is the selection of partners. Should a company deploy a corporate WAP server instead of outsourcing it from the third parties? The deployment of a WAP server is likely to be more expensive but it provides increased security and control. The company can also monitor usage closely because the server resides within the corporate premises. On the other hand, installation, maintenance and upgrades require special expertise which may be hard to find in some labor markets.

Bluetooth

Bluetooth is a short range radio technology developed to connect several devices without wires. Because of its sophisticated power consumption, it is an effective technology for a new generation of internet-capable mobile terminals. The radio link of a Bluetooth device has a range of approximately ten meters. Within ten meters, there may be up to seven devices communicating with each other with a frequency of 2400 MHz. The size of a Bluetooth chip is about 9×9 mm and the technology is able to transmit voice and data at rate of approximately 700 kbit/s. The data rate is dependant on interference from other devices (such as microwave ovens and WLAN networks), the number of Bluetooth connections in a piconet and the strength of encryption. Because it is physically small and relatively inexpensive, the chip may be built into most terminals from 2002–2003 onwards. The development of Bluetooth technology takes place within the Bluetooth Special Interest Group, consisting of over 1,000 organizations. Some members are Ericsson, Nokia, 3Com, Microsoft, Intel and IBM. According to the International Data Corporation, the US will ship 103 million Bluetooth-enabled devices in 2004 and the worldwide number will be 450 million[1].

FIGURE 1.6 ■ Homepage of Bluetooth Special Interest Group

Bluetooth enables numerous innovative services and applications which function regardless of the mobile operator. Therefore, some of the concepts and business models of Bluetooth are dangerous for mobile operators. Because the handsets are able to be used off-line in various ways, if Bluetooth penetration becomes very high, mobile operators are in danger of losing their strong position as providers of value added services and payment solutions.

Some of the solutions enabled by Bluetooth technology are:

➤ synchronization between PC and mobile handset;

➤ synchronization of two or more mobile devices;

➤ mobile payment between a cash register and a smart card inside the mobile terminal;

➤ separate mobile phone handset and a PDA using the same internet connection;

➤ separate mobile phone handset, earpiece and screen;

➤ portable speakers;

➤ mobile games between two or more players;

➤ dynamic road toll collection and subway access;

➤ ticketing services (movies, museums, amusement parks, concerts);

➤ vending machine payments;

➤ parking space payments;

➤ security services, such as office and garage access.

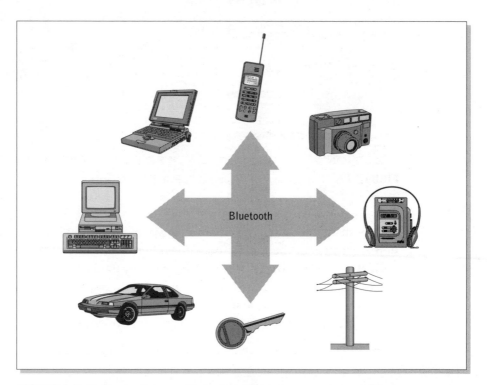

FIGURE 1.7 ■ Bluetooth is an ad hoc connection between various appliances

CASE STUDY

Socket Communications and ZIO Interactive

Socket Communications and ZIO Interactive are developing multi-player games for Pocket PC handhelds. The users are able to play interactive games at distances up to 10 meters by plugging Socket's Bluetooth Personal Network Card into the Compact Flash slot of a Pocket PC.

Strategically, Bluetooth is an important technology for mobile commerce providers coming from high street retail companies. They are able to deploy multi-channel marketing strategies combining traditional media and mobile communication into a lucrative package. With Bluetooth technology, established corporations will be able to offer new payment solutions and service concepts yet to be innovated. For example, retailers will be able to offer additional information about a particular product via a Bluetooth link located close to the actual item. This way, a customer could go "online" with his mobile terminal and acquire detailed information about the product. For instance, the customer can download a music sample from a record into his mobile phone while reading the cover. Later, at home, he could listen to the samples and download rest of the album using the fixed internet connection. This way, the traditional retail shopping experience is integrated into mobile commerce technology. In the era of electronic commerce, there is still an emotional and social need for traditional shopping.

Bluetooth technology can also be used by financial service providers such as banks and credit card companies. Visa and Ericsson have become partners in order to develop concepts and technology for mobile payment using Bluetooth technology. Additionally, Nokia has developed technology where a mobile phone, equipped with a smart card, can be used for making payments at a cash register. This way, the booming fields of mobile communication and credit cards, are approaching each other and will eventually integrate. The two core technologies, Bluetooth and smart cards, enable this integration. In the future, there might be multiple smart cards within a single mobile device. This enables a situation whereby a credit card is used for payment and loyalty points are awarded simultaneously within the same transaction.

Companies with strategic intentions to introduce Bluetooth services should closely monitor the penetration of Bluetooth-enabled mobile terminals. They will be introduced in 2001–2002. Horizontal deployment of Bluetooth services, however, will not be possible until market penetration is high enough. Consumer adoption and handset replacement cycle affect the expansion of Bluetooth-enabled terminals. Additionally, some of the first solutions are offered by the device manufacturers in order to connect physically separate pieces together. Ericsson has already introduced a mobile phone with a separate Bluetooth earpiece. It remains to be seen if these early solutions can also be used for other ad hoc Bluetooth connections.

SIM Application Toolkit and Smart Cards

SIM (Subscriber Identity Module) identifies the user of a mobile phone in GSM networks. This represents the majority of mobile phone users because the only markets not using SIMs are CDMA and TDMA networks, used particularly in the US. SIM is based on a smart card technology capable of storing and processing information. Therefore, it will be one of the main components in enabling secure mobile commerce. Although the WAP specification does not require the use of a SIM card, it provides an easier migration path to secure mobile commerce conducted using mobile devices. Furthermore, WAP Identity Module (WIM), required for storing the sensitive data and private keys of the user, is based on smart card technology. Therefore WIM can be integrated into the same card as a SIM module and the existing phones do not have to be replaced. In contrast, TDMA and CDMA phones must be equipped with smart card technology to enable secure WAP transactions conducted using WIM. Therefore, it is likely that within a couple of years, all phones will have a smart card slot for storing the user's intimate data and transactions.

SIM Application Toolkit was created in order to enable custom applications on a handset. In other words, new applications can be easily installed into a mobile phone supporting SIM Application Toolkit by replacing the SIM card. This way, a mobile operator can insert simple applications into a SIM card and distribute it directly to a customer. Additionally, an operator is able to upgrade the applications using the mobile network. The difference between the traditional SIM card and SIM Application Toolkit is the nature and role of the card usage. The SIM card was traditionally passive, providing authentication of the user at the beginning of a call. During the call, the SIM card was dormant. By contrast, SIM Application Toolkit is active, providing online and off-line applications as well as dynamic updates of them.

FIGURE 1.8 ▨ A SIM card is a tiny chip that is inserted into the smart card slot of a mobile phone

SIM Application Toolkit and WAP have some overlapping features and duplicated functionality. However, the two technologies present different sides of modern mobile development. WAP provides access to the internet and SIM Application Toolkit enables custom applications to be deployed in the mobile terminal. The development can be seen clearly in the light of PCs, where internet browsers are used to get online and programs are needed to perform off-line tasks.

SIM cards are also likely to be used in the future. The next generation SIM card, Universal SIM, is developed by an organization called 3GPP which is also responsible for 3G specifications. They further developed SIM Application Toolkit by enhancing security, application download and support for value added services. Universal SIM will be an integral part of third generation networks and terminals having databases and substantial storage capabilities.

Smart card and SIM technology are important to application developers and systems integrators who create custom applications for mobile operators and corporate customers. Mobile operators may use smart card technology to differentiate and target the services to a particular user segment. For example, a Finnish mobile operator, Radiolinja, uses SIM Application Toolkit to offer mobile and fixed internet access for teenagers. A special SIM card, including various applications, is provided with the package. The customers can read mobile e-mail and access numerous services using a mobile phone that is not WAP compliant. This way, Radiolinja is able to introduce WAP-like services before teenagers actually have the new terminals.

Smart card technology is especially important to financial institutions because it provides secure payment and authentication. Using smart cards inside the phone, banks are able to secure both online WAP payments and off-line Bluetooth transactions. Therefore, they are eagerly positioning themselves in the middle of the mobile commerce value chain. Additionally, banks have to be active in smart card technology, otherwise, mobile operators and device manufacturers may disintermediate them from the mobile commerce value chain by acquiring a direct customer relationship. The strength of financial institutions has always been their strong brand association with security and reliability. Therefore, it is logical that they also provide authentication services in the era of mobile commerce.

Micro-browsers

A micro-browser is a piece of software which enables internet access from a mobile phone. It may be installed on a SIM card with phones using SIM Application Toolkit. Another option is to integrate a micro-browser as a part of the core operating system of a mobile device. The first option enables new features to be introduced later on and gives mobile operators an opportunity to synchronize handsets at a later stage. However, most new phones are already equipped with WAP micro-browsers and, therefore, WAP software residing on a SIM card is becoming less popular.

Currently, there are three strategies on the market. Siemens, Nokia and Motorola rely on WAP. NTT DoCoMo in Japan offers HTML microbrowsers. Microsoft has taken yet another approach by offering both WAP and HTML browsers with its Mobile Explorer. NTT DoCoMo has experienced tremendous success with their service in Japan, offering packet-switched data networks along with special phones called i-Mode. One of their key success points has been a wealth of content provided by thousands of individual developers. This has been possible because i-Mode-compatible phones are capable of accessing HTML content on the internet. Naturally, the page cannot contain large images or special effects, but, as an approach, this is interesting because time to market can be cut down as developers do not have to learn another markup language. Another success factor for i-Mode has been correct pricing and convenience because they are used in a packet-switched environment where the user can connect to services instantly.

As a standard, WAP is very strong, supported by the largest players in the industry. Therefore, it seems likely that terminals equipped with a WAP-enabled browser will become more and more popular. Eventually, WML, HTML and XML evolution is likely to lead to a common standard integrating the technologies into one markup language. The industry has already announced strong support for XHTML Basic, the next generation of WAP. XHTML is supposed to lead to a common standard which brings the web and mobile worlds closer together.

Synchronization

Synchronization enables identical application data to be maintained in various devices. For example, Microsoft Exchange or Lotus Notes information on a PC can be made identical with a mobile device. Furthermore, corporate applications providing access to CRM or SCM systems can use synchronization between mobile devices and the application server. Synchronization has been particularly successful with laptop computers where connection to the internet is not always possible or takes effort. This way, the users have been able to work off-line and synchronize the information with the central system as soon as they have an opportunity to go online. The same pattern has continued with PDA (Personal Digital Assistant) devices not capable of accessing the internet directly. The off-line PDAs have dock stations connected to a PC and information can be updated as soon as the user gets back to the office.

Internet-capable mobile phones are not likely to use "traditional" off-line synchronization because of limited processing power and storage capabilities. They will be used as thin clients, accessing information in the central system through a micro-browser. This provides real-time connection to the application server and enables instant communication between the parties. For example, if the user has a new e-mail, it will be pushed to his or her mobile phone as soon as it arrives, so additional synchronization is not needed. PDA devices may use synchronization in the future because their processing power and data storage will be more developed. It will be used to update applications and data in cases where a mobile connection is more expensive than a fixed one.

Ericsson, IBM, Lotus, Motorola, Nokia, Palm Inc., Psion and Starfish Software have created an industry initiative to develop and promote a single data synchronization protocol, called SyncML. SyncML is the common language for synchronizing all devices and applications over any network. It is based on Extensible Markup Language (XML) and can be used to synchronize data in e-mail systems, calendars, contact information, to-do lists and any other applications typically used with a mobile device.

FIGURE 1.9 ■ Openwave offers its micro-browser for device manufacturers

Operating systems

The emergence of mobile internet applications and a growing demand for additional functionality has driven device manufacturers into a situation where they have to decide which operating system to deploy. Traditionally, mobile phones were used primarily for voice and simple text messages. Therefore, screens and character input methods were not regarded as important. With today's explosion of data services, however, the increased need for advanced screens and easier text input is shifting the mobile phone industry towards pen-based PDA devices more suitable for internet browsing. Additionally, third party developers must be provided with tools and open Application Programming Interfaces in order to enable custom applications to be built. Also, the existing applications, like Microsoft Exchange and Lotus Notes, will be integrated into the new mobile channel, so the operating system of a mobile device is becoming increasingly important.

Three major camps are currently competing with their mobile operating systems. The market leader, Palm OS, is distributed with Palm products and through several partnerships. Palm OS has over 130,000 registered software developers around the world. Symbian, an industry consortium consisting of Nokia, Motorola, Psion and many others, is developing an operating system called Symbian OS. It is primarily marketed for mobile phones with PC/internet connectivity and hand-held computers with advanced functionality. The third option, Microsoft Pocket PC, is integrated with other Microsoft products. It is mainly targeted at PDA manufacturers. Microsoft has also introduced a new software platform for smart phones, Smartphone 2002. Sendo, Samsung Electronics and Trium have already announced plans to build a Smartphone 2002-based phone. Along with Palm OS, Microsoft has extensive software development resources and tools around the world. Java 2 Micro Edition is an exciting option for application developers. Every device, regardless of its operating system, may run J2ME if they support the Java Runtime Environment. Therefore, Java may be used to smooth out the differences between operating systems.

Strategically, application developers and systems integrators have four main directions to choose from. They can:

> concentrate on each operating system equally;

> specialize in one of them, depending on focus areas and partners;

> develop net-centric (WAP, HTML and XHTML) applications independent of operating systems;

> focus on Java 2 Micro Edition and devices capable of running Java.

Mobile phone penetration is likely to remain higher than penetration of PDA devices because PDA devices are more expensive and target mainly business professionals. Mobile phones capable of accessing the internet are, therefore, going to be a channel for horizontal mass market applications and portals. These applications are going to be distributed with net-centric architecture, where the micro-browser is the only software component needed at the terminal. Therefore, application developers focusing on the mass market should deploy net-centric solutions independent of operating systems. In contrast, vertical business-to-business solutions are likely to be developed for PDA devices using various operating systems. Although they can be distributed with a net-centric architecture, some of the components may also be needed in the terminal. Therefore, applications with a vertical target group (CRM, logistics, transportation...) will benefit from the features of the operating system. Systems integrators and application developers concentrating on these solutions should, therefore, follow the operating system debate closely and make appropriate decisions based on future developments.

Java 2 Micro Edition (J2ME)

Sun Microsystems launched Java, its platform independent programming language and runtime environment, in 1995. Since then, the "write once, run everywhere" principle has attracted millions of application developers around the world. Sun Microsystems has been very successful in pushing Java in a variety of environments where processing power and network availability vary. To address the needs of various operating systems and environments, Java technologies have been divided into three editions:

➤ Java 2 Enterprise Edition (J2EE).

➤ Java 2 Standard Edition (J2SE).

➤ Java 2 Micro Edition (J2ME).

Each edition provides developers with tools that can be used to design and implement applications for a range of devices.

The market potential of J2ME technology is enormous, because suitable devices range from tiny smart cards to TV set-top boxes. In between, there are pagers, smart phones, PDAs, communicators, car systems and several other emerging consumer devices. The architecture of J2ME consists of:

➤ KVM (K Virtual Machine) or JVM (Java Virtual Machine);

➤ configurations;

➤ profiles;

➤ Java language.

The K Virtual Machine is used in small, resource-constrained devices because it can run on only 160KB of memory. The Java Virtual Machine can be used in devices delivering more processing power but less than that of a standard PC. PDAs, set-top boxes, communicators and car devices fall into this category. In addition to the Virtual Machine, configurations and profiles are used to define device characteristics. At the moment, there are two configurations: J2ME Connected Device Configuration (CDC) and J2ME Connected Limited Device Configuration (CLDC). CDC runs on top of the Java Virtual Machine and CLDC on top of the K Virtual Machine because it is designed for devices with limited resources. Profiles are probably one of the most interesting components for application developers because they include information about user interfaces, storage and networking. PDA profile, for example, could be used to define screen size, input methods and storage capability of a Personal Digital Assistant. This way, the application developer does not have to implement these details at the code level.

J2ME is an interesting technology because it has the potential to become the de facto standard of mobile application development. It may be used to download games and dynamic system upgrades over the network, install extra applications into the mobile device and define the graphical user interface of the terminal. In a

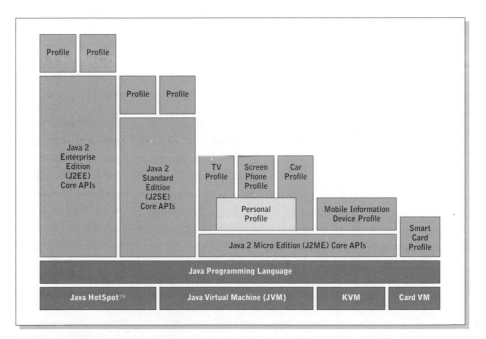

FIGURE 1.10 ■ J2ME technology has implemented profiles that can be used to define the characteristics of the user terminal   Source: Sun Microsystems

way, J2ME brings stability in a market situation where application developers do not know what will be the most important operating system of the future. Every device, regardless of operating system, may run J2ME applications if a Java Virtual Machine is supported. This reduces the importance of the operating system as applications run on top of the Virtual Machine, not directly on the operating system.

Today, most of the important market players support Java. Symbian has ported J2ME to the Symbian OS operating environment. Ericsson, Nokia, Palm Computing, Samsung and NTT DoCoMo have all licensed the J2ME specification. It remains to be seen how the penetration of J2ME supported devices will develop. From 2002 onwards, these devices will enter the mass market and it may take another year or two before the development of horizontal, mass market J2ME applications is encouraged. In the meantime, application developers should pay close attention to J2ME and focus on vertical solutions where Java Virtual Machine is installed on Palm, Pocket PC and Symbian OS devices.

Mobile networks: GSM

General Packet Radio Service (GPRS)

GPRS is a packet-switched protocol offering instant internet access and enhanced data capabilities to existing GSM networks. It requires a software upgrade, new cards in the base station, and two pieces of equipment to handle the internet connection on the mobile operator's side. Additionally, consumers require new mobile terminals in order to use the new services.

GPRS uses the existing time slots of GSM networks to provide data services. Therefore, the service level is dependent on the amount of voice traffic and the number of active connections. In an ideal environment with little or no voice traffic, GPRS is able to use seven or eight time slots for data transfer. This way, the connection speed could realistically reach 115 Kbit/s. However, the initial speed for GPRS implementations is likely to remain as low as 43.2 Kbit/s downstream and 14.4 Kbit/s upstream. The speed may be even lower than that because of immature user terminals. In the second phase, the connection speed may increase to bi-directional 56 Kbit/s. These figures are substantially lower than the hyped 171 Kbit/s which is the theoretical burst transmission speed of a GPRS network with no voice traffic.

Despite the hype and false expectations, GPRS has the potential to revolutionize mobile internet access. As a matter of fact, the small screen size of mobile terminals and the light structure of markup language (WAP or XHTML) enable innovative services without high transmission speed. The most relevant success factors of GPRS-enabled terminals are instant connectivity and continual connection with the network. Because it is a packet-switched network, data can be pushed to a mobile terminal. Therefore, the user is able to receive an e-mail as soon as it hits the inbox. Compared to the old circuit-switched (GSM) networks, this is more convenient. The user does not have to make a data call to check for e-mail. Another advantage of packet-switched networks is a new payment model whereby the user pays for the transferred data, not for the online time. Almost all the WAP applications require data to be transferred in bursts as opposed to continuously. Therefore, there are periods of inactivity in between the data bursts. For example, when browsing financial news the user downloads a certain amount of data from the network and then reads the screen. When compared to circuit-switched networks, GPRS is cost effective because the customer pays only for data transferred, not for the time taken to read the news.

Enhanced Data Rates for Global Evolution (EDGE)

EDGE is another packet-switched evolution of the existing GSM networks. It boosts the bandwidth of GPRS networks up to 384 Kbit/s. This speed is achieved by using all eight 48 Kbit/s timeslots available in the network. Realistically, however, the speed mobile operators are able to offer to customers is likely to be around 40 Kbit/s upstream and 100 Kbit/s downstream. Even though EDGE depends on GPRS equipment to provide service, mobile operators may choose an option to update the existing GSM networks directly to EDGE. This way, the operator would have to wait for technology to become available. The first installations of EDGE are expected to take place in 2002 at the earliest. Therefore, a direct migration path to EDGE may be a selection for conservative operators wanting to see how the market for data services performs. In addition, GSM operators have to make strategic decisions regarding new networks because they aim to maximize service life and minimize costs. This can be done by selecting the correct network standards instead of investing in all of them as they become available. When compared with 3G, the next generation of mobile networks, EDGE is similar in terms of bandwidth and timing. Some mobile operators without licenses for 3G are likely to retain EDGE and wait for the new technologies instead of rushing to 3G. For operators, this might be a viable strategy because the demand for high speed data has not been completely proven.

Wideband CDMA (WCDMA) or 3G

Wideband CDMA, being a part of the Universal Mobile Telecommunication System (UMTS), is a third generation mobile network capable of transferring multimedia between terminals. Implementation cost for a mobile operator is high because the network has to be redesigned and new equipment is needed at the base stations. 3G licence costs have also been very expensive to operators, especially in Europe. Additionally, consumers require new mobile terminals in order to access WCDMA services.

The speed of WCDMA networks has been highly exaggerated. Most consumers associate the new networks with a capacity of 2 Mbit/s. Therefore, the initial bandwidth, being similar to EDGE (40 Kbit/s upstream and 100 Kbit/s downstream), will be a disappointment to the markets. Maximum speeds of 100 Kbit/s upstream and 384 Kbit/s downstream will be achieved at a later stage. However, higher speeds are likely to cost more and initially they will only be offered in metropolitan areas. Therefore, light solutions capable of delivering information to a handset with less bandwidth are still likely to be killer applications in the era of WCDMA.

Large scale implementation of WCDMA will take place in 2003 at the earliest. Compared to EDGE, WCDMA does not offer significant improvement of transmission speed. However, the voice capacity is more extensive and WCDMA networks are able to offer scalable network infrastructure.

Mobile networks: CDMA

While GSM and TDMA operators around the world are going to deploy the technology defined earlier (GPRS – EDGE – WCDMA), CDMA operators are likely to choose another path. This is a consequence of different technology used in CDMA and its natural migration path towards high speed mobile networks capable of transferring packet-switched data. Most CDMA operators come from North America, but there are also countries using this technology in Asia. Globally, CDMA technology is substantially smaller than GSM in terms of subscriber base and a number of supporting operators. Geographically, however, it is important in the United States.

cdmaOne (IS-95A)

cdmaOne is the first commercial version of CDMA, currently in use by North American mobile operators. It is based on IS-95A-standards and can be optimized for circuit-switched data capable of transferring 14.4 Kbit/s. These data capabilities can be introduced with the use of software overlay. Most mobile operators have already implemented circuit-switched data services in their networks.

IS-95B

cdmaOne networks may be upgraded to support packet-switched data with transmission speeds up to 84 Kbit/s. However, the operators introducing the new services, based on IS-95B-standards, are more likely to support data transmission at 64 Kbit/s. CDMA operators are required to install new software in order to support the enhanced data capabilities. In addition to increased speed of data transfer, voice capacity of the network is improved. However, the major implication of IS-95B is that the data is transferred in packets. This way, the WAP services will experience a substantial increase in convenience and service level. The charging models are also likely to be changed in favor of the consumer. IS-95B is an interim technology between the old networks and more advanced technologies. Therefore, some operators are likely to skip IS-95B and proceed directly to the next level by 1XRTT.

2.5G for CDMA (1XRTT)

For CDMA operators, 1XRTT is a significant move towards advanced high speed data networks. In addition to increased voice capacity, it offers an initial data transmission speed of up to 153 Kbit/s enabling sophisticated internet applications. At a later stage, 1XRTT will be capable of transferring data at a speed of 307 Kbit/s. The name "2.5G for CDMA" comes from the characteristics of a 1XRTT network. While it is not a fully compliant third generation mobile network, it is much more developed than the existing second generation networks. Therefore, 1XRTT resides somewhere in between 2G and 3G.

In order to deploy 1XRTT, mobile operators must renew channel cards, chips and software. This is a substantial investment but some of the same components may be used when migrating to the next level networks, called cdma2000.

cdma2000 (3XRTT)

3XRTT, commercially called cdma2000, is the ultimate goal for numerous CDMA operators. Similar to the WCDMA of the GSM operators, cdma2000 is another path to the Universal Mobile Communication System (UMTS). Eventually, WCDMA and cdma2000 are likely to merge creating a global mobile network, where a single phone may be used regardless of geographical location.

cdma2000 is able to transfer data with a speed of 384 Kbit/s. In order to implement the new network, mobile operators are required to update the software and acquire new channel cards.

Wireless LAN – Another Perspective Towards 3G

WLAN (Wireless Local Area Network) technology was not an issue of discussion until European operators ended up paying enormous amounts of money for 3G spectrum licenses. After that, the stock prices of operators have decreased substantially, partly because of general technology slowdown and partly because investors think that 3G spectrum holders are in danger of drifting towards financial crises. This is caused by heavy investment in third generation network infrastructure and license fees that had to be paid in advance. In this situation, operators without 3G licenses are actively looking for alternative ways to offer sophisticated mobile services with smaller investment.

In a way, WLAN technology is closer to the fundamental principle of the internet, where everybody can set up an individual network as long as it follows the general internet guidelines. Therefore, internet Service Providers have shown an increasing interest towards WLAN technology. Similarly to the internet, WLAN networks cannot provide consistent Quality of Service (QoS). Because they operate in a free, "polluted" frequency band, other devices such as microwave ovens, Bluetooth devices and cordless phones produce interference and may cause lower service levels at times.

Generally, WLAN service providers do not have to pay spectrum license fees, because they operate in the license-exempt 2.4 GHz and 5 GHz frequency bands. France and the UK are exceptions to the prevailing frequency policy as they have imposed more restrictive procedures. According to the Wireless Telegraphy Act 1998, private (homes and companies, indoors) WLAN networks operating on the 2.4 GHz band do not require licenses in the UK. A Telecommunications Act License is required to offer third party WLAN access. Currently, the Government does not have a formal process in place to issue commercial licenses. It is currently not known how the UK will react to the new WLAN technology using the 5 GHz frequency band. In France, the frequency band for WLAN applications is limited. In addition, Agence Nationale des Frequences (ANFR) has limited the maximum permitted radiated power in products, making it impossible to offer WLAN services outdoors. Despite limitations, some companies are offering commercial WLAN services in France, such as US-based Waypoint, which is building WLANs for luxury hotels.

Currently, the WLAN market is dominated by equipment based on the IEEE 802.11b standard. IEEE 802.11b defines wireless local area networking using the 2.4 GHz frequency band between a client network interface card (NIC) and an access point. The access point can be connected to a wired local area network or internet access gateway. IEEE 802.11b compatible networks are able to deliver bandwidths up to 11 Mbit/s, but the realistic data rate is closer to 5 Mbit/s. Compared to 384 kbit/s provided by 3G networks, WLAN performs over ten times faster. Bandwidth depends on the following issues:

➤ distance between a WLAN card and an access point;

➤ encryption methods;

➤ interference from other devices using the same frequency band;

➤ number of WLAN cards attached to the same access point.

The maximum range for IEEE 802.11b equipment is approximately 50–100 meters indoors and 300–500 meters outdoors using an omni-directional antenna. WLAN can be used to provide internet access via:

➤ "hot spots", located indoors in office buildings, restaurants, train stations, airports, hotels, shopping centers, etc.;

➤ outdoor access points in densely populated areas.

The coverage area of a WLAN access point is much less than the area covered by one 3G base station. Therefore, WLAN is not a direct competitor to 3G mobile networks. The game becomes interesting when an operator without a 3G license deploys a hybrid network using GPRS, EDGE and WLAN technology. In this case, the operator is able to offer advanced services without having to pay license fees.

By the end of 2002, the next generation of WLAN products is expected to be available. These products will use the license-exempt 5 GHz band and they will be designed to be more robust against sources of interference. Bandwidth in next generation WLAN products will increase as the maximum physical rate is 54 Mbit/s, providing a practical data speed of up to 32–38 Mbit/s.

There are two competing standards with the next generation WLAN market: IEEE 802.11a and HiperLAN/2. HiperLAN/2, approved by European Telecommunications Standards Institute (ETSI), has been developed primarily in Europe. US-backed IEEE 802.11a standard relies on earlier development of IEEE 802.11b and, therefore, products supporting this standard are likely to be introduced first. Both standards may be used to complement or compete with the third generation network technology in case an operator decides to build a hybrid network, using both WLAN and GPRS/EDGE/UMTS.

Standard	Frequency	Maximum range	Practical data rate
IEEE 802.11b	2.4 GHz	30–100 meters indoors 100–500 meters outdoors	5 Mbit/s
IEEE 802.11a	5 GHz	30–100 meters indoors, 100–500 meters outdoors	32–38 Mbit/s
HiperLAN/2	5 GHz	30–100 meters indoors 100–500 meters outdoors	32–38 Mbit/s
Bluetooth	2.4 GHz	10–100 meters	Asymmetric 721 Kbit/s downstream and 57.6 Kbit/s upstream, Symmetric 432.6 Kbit/s

FIGURE 1.11 ■ WLAN standards compared to Bluetooth. Note that practical data rates and maximum range depend on several issues, such as interference, encryption and number of connections per access point

The availability of user terminals is one of the big questions for WLAN technology. Currently, laptop computers and some PDA devices can be attached to a WLAN network using a CF or a PCMCIA card. In future, we are likely to see PDAs and mobile phones that support multiple network technologies. From a consumer point of view, network technologies should be transparent and roaming between WLAN access points and 3G base stations should take place automatically.

CASE STUDY

Hybrid WLAN/GPRS network provided by Jippii

In Finland, an internet Service Provider, Jippii, has announced plans to launch a hybrid WLAN/GPRS network, offering roaming between a WLAN and the countrywide GPRS network. Wireless Network Services (WNS), a subsidiary of Jippii, will provide the network infrastructure. WNS has plans to deploy over 400 base stations by the end of 2001 and 900 by the end of 2003.

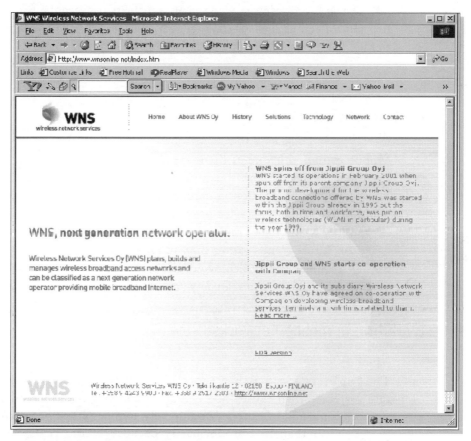

FIGURE 1.12 ■ WNS, a subsidiary of a Finnish ISP, is offering broadband access to the internet using WLAN technology

Testing UMTS-WLAN integration

Ericsson and a Norwegian operator, Telenor, are testing the practical and commercial aspects of integrating WLAN networks and UMTS. UMTS users may access WLAN seamlessly as they enter crowded hot spots such as airports or conference areas.

The project, called H2U, will focus on connecting a HiperLAN/2 network to the surrounding UMTS network with seamless mobility between the two. This way, the strengths of both technologies are brought together: the wide coverage of UMTS and the greater bandwidth of HiperLAN2 for crowded hot spots.

Mobile evolution

Mobile evolution is one of the most important issues in understanding the customer behavior and business requirements of mobile commerce. Regardless of their position in the mobile commerce value chain, all the companies participating in service provisioning should closely follow the progress of enabling technologies and solutions. This way, strategic decisions can be based on future trends rather than today's technology. By studying correct timing, companies can also avoid market entry too early or too late which causes additional costs and anxiety among investors.

Evolution in mobile networks

North America

The North American mobile network market is characterized by three separate systems which causes fragmentation and slower uptake of mobile data services compared to Europe. Additionally, mobile phone penetration is likely to be slower than in Europe, partly because of the "called party pays" approach. Therefore, the culture of mobile communication has not developed as fast as in Europe. The network evolution discussed in this chapter is based on CDMA technology. TDMA and GSM are covered in the next chapter.

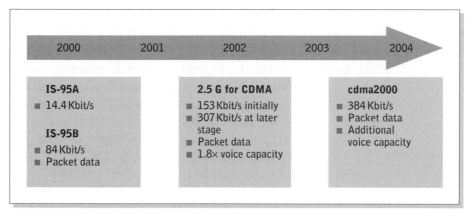

FIGURE 1.13 ■ Evolution for CDMA

As seen in the figure, packet-switched networks are already commercially available in North America. However, most operators skip IS-95B and proceed directly to 1XRTT networks. They will be available roughly in 2001 but penetration and coverage will take time before mass market applications may be implemented. In addition, networks are initially built only in metropolitan areas. The rest of the country has to use the old networks. 1XRTT will be closely followed by cdma2000 in 2003. Because new client terminals are needed before cdma2000-enabled services can be used, wider deployment of 3G services is likely to take place in 2004–2006.

3G terminal penetration is greatly dependent on the following issues:

➤ terminal cost;
➤ cost of the services;
➤ mobile device replacement cycle;
➤ general economy in North America;
➤ marketing;
➤ competing technologies, such as WLAN coverage in major cities and terminals supporting them.

The internet has developed tremendously during the last five years. New access methods and applications have been spurred with the development of technology. If we look five years ahead, it is very hard to say which technology and access methods will prevail. Therefore, it should be remembered that new, competing technologies may be used to replace 3G networks. For example, what happens if WLAN technology, especially HiperLAN, capable of delivering substantially higher speeds, rises and competes with the 3G networks? There are already PDA devices and mobile phones supporting WLANs. The question, in this case, is the matter of coverage. WLAN cannot cover the wide areas that 3G base stations can. However, in highly urbanized countries, only a small percentage of the land area has to be covered to reach 90–95 per cent of the population. Therefore, WLAN connectivity may be used in the future for connecting wireless terminals using high data speed and voice over IP (VoIP).

Rest of the world

GSM and TDMA evolution follow the same patterns. While TDMA is used primarily in North America, GSM is offered by more than half of all the mobile operators in the world. Therefore, most of the attention is naturally on GSM evolution and the services enabled by the enhanced connectivity and speed. Mobile operators considering the new network technologies aim to maximize the operational time of a network and minimize the expenses regarding implementation and future migration path. Additionally, the markets are different in various countries and the implementation of the new technologies is dependent on customer adoption, mobile terminal penetration and the market outlook in general. It is natural that operators take a different approach in conservative, small markets without the critical mass of data users than in advanced, high-potential markets.

In short, the factors affecting the deployment of the future network technologies are:

- mobile phone penetration at the moment;
- the future potential of mobile terminal owners;
- the users of data services now;
- future potential for data services;
- competitor strategies;
- historical success;
- general market/economy situation.

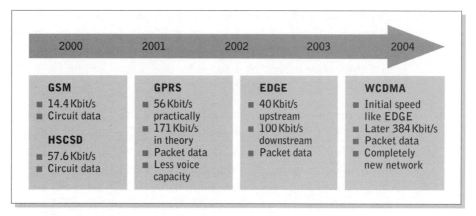

FIGURE 1.14 ■ Evolution of GSM networks

Mobile operators may choose to skip one or more technologies to save money and wait for the market to develop. In addition, the demand for data services has not been fully proven yet. Some conservative operators take a strategic direction to stay in the background and see how the markets welcome newcomers. In case the markets adopt the new data services, they implement the next technology in line. In contrast, some operators believe in low speed data services offered in a packet-switched environment. Therefore, they implement GPRS as soon as possible, but prefer not to upgrade the networks immediately after that to support EDGE. The operator has time to see how the markets will develop before purchasing third generation WCDMA networks with high data transmission speeds.

GSM and TDMA operators have five possible routes ahead of them:

➤ install GPRS, EDGE and WCDMA as soon as they become commercially available;

➤ skip GPRS to proceed directly to EDGE and WCDMA;

➤ skip both GPRS and EDGE to proceed to WCDMA;

➤ install GPRS and proceed directly to WCDMA;

➤ install GPRS and EDGE as soon as they become commercially available. No WCDMA installation, because the operator does not have a license. Operators without 3G licenses are also likely to explore the possibilities of WLAN networks.

The strategies of mobile operators are highly dependent on market outlook and the availability of new networks. Additionally, implementation depends on the availability of the terminals supporting the new features. So far, it seems that the major delays are caused by late arrival of handsets rather than the availability of the networks.

Application developers, systems integrators and content providers are strongly affected by the emergence of the new, high speed networks. However, they should bear in mind that the real bandwidth which mobile operators are likely to introduce, especially at the initial stage, is going to be substantially lower than the hyped numbers. For example, first GPRS solutions are able to transfer data with a speed of 43.2 Kbit/s downstream and 14.4 Kbit/s upstream. This is significantly less than the early assumptions of 171 Kbit/s. Theoretically, 171 Kbit/s is achieved when all the time slots of GSM network are used for data. This leaves no room for voice traffic, which is an absurd situation because voice is still likely to be the major application in the era of data services. Additionally, most operators are likely to increase the cost of high speed transmission. Therefore, content and applications capable of delivering value added services with less bandwidth are well positioned at the initial stage of the new, packet-switched mobile networks. Solutions with high potential are those integrating location and personalization technology into instant messaging.

Evolution in mobile terminals

The development of mobile terminals is partly dependent on the evolution of the networks. Therefore, companies aware of new network features are better able to understand the market situation. Given that the initial bandwidth is substantially lower than previously expected, advanced features, like videotelephony and mobile movie provisioning, are likely to be launched on a large scale in 2005 at the earliest. However, bandwidth is not the only feature that narrows down potential applications. Network-based location services are also dependent on the equipment installed by the mobile operator. Some location technologies provide the location of a handset with precision of 100 meters while others rely on cell-based location ranging from 150 meters to several kilometers in accuracy. Location technologies are especially important with the evolution of car navigation systems which use network and satellite-dependent positioning. Mobile terminals inside the car are able to use both technologies in order to provide driving directions and information on special points of interest.

Another factor affecting the evolution of mobile handsets is consumer adoption. It remains to be seen how the advanced features are welcomed by the end users. While mobile networks are primarily moving into a direction to provide high speed data services, it has not been proven how consumers will relate to the new applications. Additionally, positive or negative consumer adoption has an impact on the mobile handset replacement cycle which, in turn, relates to the deployment of the new solutions.

In the light of fixed internet expansion, mobile internet terminals have a realistic chance to become mass market devices. Mobile terminals are likely to be more convenient and easier to use than PCs. They are also cheaper or completely subsidized by the mobile operators. Also, the users of the mobile internet are already familiar with fixed internet applications. The chances for fast consumer adoption are good.

By 2003, there will be more mobile handsets accessing the internet than PCs. According to the Yankee Group, internet-enabled phone users are expected to reach 204 million by 2005. Additionally, the Gartner Group forecasts that by 2004, more than 40 per cent of business-to-consumer e-commerce transactions outside North America will be made over a wireless phone.[2]

The evolution of mobile terminals will be characterized by customer segmentation. Handsets focusing on a narrow target group, such as teens, construction workers or business professionals, have specific requirements in terms of functions and applications. Business professionals require efficient time management and team working capabilities. Teens may choose a handset with a built-in game console. Construction workers may rely on a water resistant phone covered with rubber. Therefore, customer segmentation will be a crucial part of the future and device manufacturers have to develop several models in order to stay in the business.

Consumer electronics and mobile communication come closer to each other by integrating new technologies with handsets. In some cases, mobile handset owners can already use their device as a calculator, MP3 player, radio, remote control or game console. Naturally, devices with the biggest potential are those integrating a mobile phone with another mobile device such as music player or game console. This way, the portability of the two devices is used to create totally new service concepts.

As noted earlier, increased capabilities of mobile networks enable new terminals with an instant internet connection. Therefore, user requirements for the handsets are likely to be changed. Traditionally, small mobile phones, used primarily for voice communication, have been favored because they fit in the pocket and are more portable. Now, with the emergence of data services, it is likely that the size of a mobile terminal is going to be increased. This is natural, as the use of internet applications requires a bigger screen and more flexible character input methods. Therefore, today's PDA devices, focused for business professionals, may well become everybody's preferred mobile terminal. Naturally, there will also be people who use a mobile handset solely for voice communication. Then size of a mobile phone is still one of the most important criteria for purchase.

The strong potential of PDA devices has already been noticed by device manufacturers. Therefore, companies develop aggressive operating systems suitable for the future terminals. The main reason for this is the increased demands for third party applications. The flexible operating system of a PDA terminal enables application developers to create custom applications for several user segments. Therefore, one of the characteristics of mobile terminal evolution is a trend towards generic operating systems supported by a large number of companies.

Bluetooth is a technology capable of changing the evolution of mobile terminals. If it becomes commercially widespread, the price of a Bluetooth chip decreases substantially, resulting in new, innovative use of this short-range radio link. Bluetooth can be used to connect physically separate pieces together without wires. A mobile phone, PDA and earpiece may be separate units, so the user doesn't have to carry a PDA while making a telephone call. An earpiece can also be used conveniently because no wires are necessary.

However, the biggest impact of Bluetooth technology is yet to come. With mass market Bluetooth services, customers are able to pay using a smart card inside the phone when they drive into a car wash. They can open a garage door by typing a security code into their mobile phone. When they get home, the same phone can be used to control domestic appliances and synchronize data between the PC and the mobile terminal. This way, the mobile handset can be used, not only for making a telephone call, but also for numerous other duties in everyday life. Therefore, the ultimate evolution of a mobile phone results in a device capable of accessing the internet and processing payment transactions, together with numerous other tasks.

TABLE 1.2 ■ Predicted evolution of mobile networks

	Current	Future
Screens and text input	■ Black and white ■ Small screens ■ Keypad for inserting text	■ Color ■ Bigger screens ■ Pen-based text input, speech recognition at the later stage
Handset size and purpose	■ Small mobile phones with small screens ■ Voice is the dominant application ■ Communicators with enhanced screens and text input	■ Generally, the size of a handset will increase because of bigger screens and more flexible text input methods. ■ Increased importance in data services
Target group	■ Mass market phones with some exceptions	■ Increased segmentation ■ New features and technologies according to target groups (MP3 player, gameboy, GPS receiver)
Bluetooth	■ Separate phone and earpiece	■ Payment solutions (vending machines, road toll collection, tickets, parking) ■ Security services ■ Mobile games ■ Synchronization ■ Domestic appliance control
Security	■ WAP Identity Module (WIM) in GSM phones	■ Several solutions based on smart card technology
Operating systems	■ Most of the phones have proprietary operating systems, WAP microbrowsers are entering the market ■ PDA devices have Symbian OS, Palm OS or Microsoft Pocket PC as an operating system.	■ There will be general trend towards third party operating systems and microbrowsers. ■ Microbrowsers (WAP, HTML and XHTML) will become a part of the operating system
Performance	■ Little processing power ■ Limited data storage capabilities	■ More processing power and enhanced storage capabilities within the devices ■ Universal SIM cards in 3G phones including small databases and extensive data storage capability

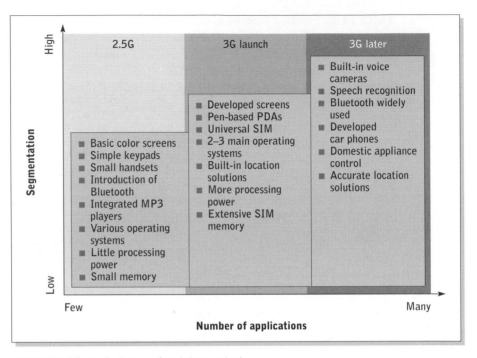

High

2.5G 3G launch 3G later

Segmentation

Built-in voice
cameras
Speech recognition
Bluetooth widely
used
Developed
car phones
Domestic appliance
control
Accurate location
solutions

Developed screens
Pen-based PDAs
Universal SIM
2–3 main operating
systems
Built-in location
solutions
More processing
power
Extensive SIM
memory

Basic color screens
Simple keypads
Small handsets
Introduction of
Bluetooth
Integrated MP3
players
Various operating
systems
Little processing
power
Small memory

Low

Few Many

Number of applications

FIGURE 1.15 ▪ Evolution of mobile terminals

Evolution in applications

Evolution of mobile applications is, without a doubt, a controversial issue. Similar to the fixed internet, future expectations have been set with multimedia and mobile videotelephony being the ultimate goal. However, reports of the fixed internet have already proved that multimedia itself is not used by many people. There are e-mail, chat and other less sophisticated programs that are killer applications instead of streaming multimedia. Therefore, it is likely that mobile internet will follow the same pattern, with stripped-down features. Completely new solutions will also revolutionize the use of mobile internet. To sum up, high bandwidth is not always needed to offer sophisticated services capable of providing added value to the customer.

Evolution in applications is highly dependent on the development of mobile terminals. Operating system, screen size and the data processing capability of a mobile device define the framework for the application. Additionally, the type of micro-browser and possible plug-ins limit the applications provided over the network. Application developers should work closely with device manufacturers in order to understand the requirements of the future.

Mobile terminals are a challenging environment for an application developer because of the variety of screen sizes and data processing capabilities. Especially at the initial stage, the processing power of mobile devices is substantially lower than computers. Screen sizes are not standardized, which makes it very hard to develop applications that look ideal in all devices. Content and graphical layout have to be separated from each other. This is the only way to optimize layout and ensure that the device is capable of receiving all the data that has been transmitted.

At the initial stage, most of the data services provided by mobile portals are general news and entertainment. However, news and entertainment will fall short of achieving customer loyalty because the competition in mobile services is fierce. Therefore, the portal sites will offer messaging solutions, such as e-mail, to increase customer loyalty and reduce churn. In addition to offering mobile messaging services, companies will move towards personalization to overcome the limitations in screen size and character input. This way the customers are able to access relevant services and information without expensive and time consuming browsing. After personalization, some application developers will introduce large scale location solutions integrating information into location coordinates. With location technology, mobile portal providers are able to offer new value added services to customers. Those services are discussed in detail in Chapter 5: Location-based services.

Application business models are also likely to change with the development of new mobile terminals. Currently, the user pays for access to the mobile internet personally. In the future, location-based and personalized advertisement will take place, gradually offering subsidized voice and data services. A mobile terminal, being a personal device, is an ideal tool for target marketing. There are already some companies offering free voice calls in return for listening to targeted advertising messages. However, mobile advertising is not likely to be introduced on a large scale until terminals develop and networks are able to offer location information in a relatively precise manner.

Evolution also takes place in other horizontal applications, such as commerce and messaging. Mobile commerce will develop in terms of security, personalization and time sensitivity. Financial institutions will launch smart payment cards that can be included in the phone. This way, the security of a transaction is enhanced and convenient payment solutions can be launched. Additionally, mobile shopping will be characterized by personal matters and time sensitivity. It is impossible to "surf" the mobile internet in the same way we do using the fixed internet. Therefore, successful merchants have to introduce convenient solutions for personalization. In a personalized environment, the customer can access applications and information easily without time consuming searching. Time sensitivity and independence of location will make mobile commerce unique from all the other marketing channels. Customers can complete transactions regardless of their location or time. Instant messaging technology and commerce applications will gradually integrate, offering solutions for mobile commerce. For example, a customer may set limits on a certain stock price in his personal portfolio. After the limits are broken, an instant message is automatically sent to his mobile terminal. While reading the message, he may decide to sell or buy some stocks, immediately, using his mobile device.

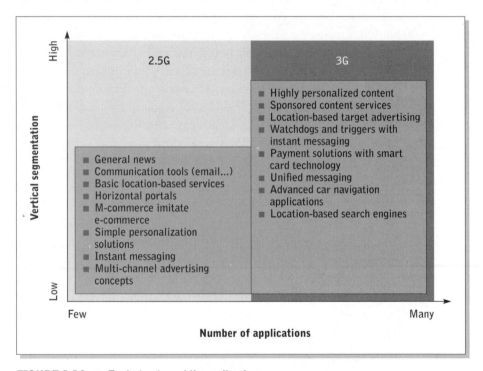

FIGURE 1.16 ■ Evolution in mobile applications

In addition to the evolution of instant messaging, messaging in general will develop. Unified messaging will integrate the various channels into one service, accessible from any device. With a unified messaging solution, the customer is able to read e-mail, access a voice mailbox and receive faxes using a variety of channels. Theoretically, the customer would also be able to send faxes, e-mails and other messages from any device, including a mobile terminal. Obviously, the key technology in the development of unified messaging is text-to-speech and speech-to-text transformation.

In conclusion, it seems inevitable that application developers and systems integrators are in a key position to develop the mobile services of the future. It is not merely the question of bandwidth, since most of the services described above may be offered with relatively low speed. It is also a question of systems integration. Therefore, the evolution of mobile applications will not only develop according to the framework given by future network technologies, but also according to possibilities and limitations of back-end systems.

TABLE 1.3 ■ Potential development for mobile applications

	Current	Future
Target group	■ Horizontal mass market applications	■ Vertical applications with target groups ■ User segmentation
Commerce applications	■ Mobile commerce tries unsuccessfully to imitate e-commerce business models	■ Multi-channel strategies ■ Location-based shopping ■ Increased personalization ■ Time-sensitive premium services ■ Bluetooth-enabled transactions ■ Increased importance in systems integration
Messaging	■ Mobile e-mail ■ SMS	■ Advanced instant messaging ■ Unified messaging combining all the messaging applications together ■ Increased time sensitivity
Advertising	■ Mobile advertising is virtually nonexistent	■ Sponsored content ■ Location-based advertising ■ Free voice calls in return for listening to advertisements ■ Personalized advertising
Corporate applications	■ Simple CRM, ERP and SCM applications	■ The corporate applications are integrated into mobile technologies resulting in location-based applications and increased time sensitivity with instant messaging

Evolution in consumer behavior

Consumers have the power to determine successful applications and terminal concepts, so their expectations have to be examined and nurtured. However, some of the applications and service models which exist today are so unusual that it was impossible to forecast consumer demand for them. Text messaging is one of the surprising successes, bringing additional revenue to mobile operators and application developers. Who could have expected that messages typed with a very slow, 12-key keyboard would have such a success among mobile phone users? In Finland, the revenue from text messages already exceeds the revenue generated from television advertising, not to mention banner advertising on the internet. Imagine the same thing happening in the US, Germany or some other country with a large population.

However, evolution in consumer behavior can be broadly predicted by examining the success factors of yesterday. Communication is likely to remain one of the core reasons for using a mobile device. The beginning of the internet was also characterized by a strong emphasis on communication tools, such as e-mail and newsgroups. E-mail has been able to maintain its strong position through the evolution of the fixed internet. Therefore, it seems inevitable that tools that provide social communication between family members, business professionals and friends are likely to conquer the mobile internet as well.

Any development is partly dependent on the evolution of mobile networks because advanced solutions require the implementation of sophisticated location technologies. Where evolution continues to be focused on communication tools, there will be solutions that are based on the location of a handset. For example, family members are able to communicate with each other based on their current position. This way, the core characteristics (time sensitivity, location, intimacy) of mobile phones are used to innovate new communication services.

The evolution in consumer behavior always depends on the price of the services. The third generation networks are associated with mobile multimedia and videotelephony. However, their increased bandwidth is likely to cost substantially more than applications requiring less speed. Therefore, mobile multimedia for a horizontal target group cannot succeed unless the price is acceptable to the consumers. In contrast, business users are likely to be less concerned about the price. Additional value provided by the new technology is the most important factor for them.

Consumer behavior is also affected by the business models of mobile operators. In some countries the mobile terminals are subsidized and the consumer pays, primarily, for network connection. This way the mobile operator can affect the adoption of the new services by providing new terminals to the consumers. The third generation networks are able to accelerate consumer adoption by delivering devices supporting advanced applications. In addition, mobile operators can offer free trials for videotelephony and other sophisticated services. The situation is different in countries where subsidization is not used. The price of multimedia terminals is likely to be high initially, but those making a purchase decision will definitely use the advanced services. This is different from the countries with subsidized terminals, where there are no guarantees that consumers will actually start to use the new services when they are given the terminal for free. All in all, the mobile terminal replacement cycle will most definitely affect the implementation and deployment of the new services enabled by the advanced mobile networks.

What is the difference between the fixed and the mobile internet?

Mobile and fixed internet are very different in terms of form factor, business models and industry characteristics. Therefore, companies aiming to deploy mobile internet services should reconsider many of electronic commerce's best practices to be able to take into consideration the characteristics of mobile devices.

Form factor

The fixed internet is used primarily for communication, entertainment and getting information about a particular point of interest. Typically, the user has a screen of 17 inches and a network connection providing data with a speed ranging from 56 Kbit/s to several megabits. The computer is likely to have more processing power than is needed to use the services available on the internet. In addition, most of the information can be saved on a hard disk to be used later, while off-line. The user has two devices in order to give commands to the computer: a keyboard and a mouse. Reading news and communicating with friends is easy with the equipment described above.

Mobile phones are different. Connection speed is substantially lower and screens are able to support only a couple of rows of text. Black and white images can be displayed, but low quality and limited screen size raises questions about whether they are able to bring any added value to mobile services. Compared to PCs, the processing power of mobile phones and PDA devices is very low and data storage cannot be used to maintain masses of information. Additionally, character input methods are slower and require time to get comfortable. Therefore, mobile terminals are not likely to be used for internet surfing the way we understand it today.

Application developers and other parties creating solutions for the mobile internet have to acknowledge the limitations of mobile terminals. Mobile operators, content providers and device manufacturers should manage consumer expectations in an appropriate way or there will be huge disappointment when consumers realize that their expectations were not met. A mobile phone will never be the "internet in your pocket" in the way we understand fixed internet. Therefore, totally new services and business concepts will emerge as mobile terminal penetration increases and companies understand the limitations of the devices.

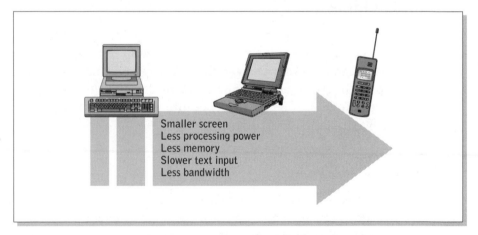

Smaller screen
Less processing power
Less memory
Slower text input
Less bandwidth

FIGURE 1.17 ■ Mobile phones and PCs come from two different worlds

The mobile internet should not be regarded as equal to the PC-based internet. There are many features of a fixed internet connection that mobile devices cannot replace. The two will always co-exist, providing additional features to each other. For example, some location-based services will have a web interface for additional functionality. Furthermore, web auction sites are likely to launch mobile extensions to their existing services to increase time sensitivity and the excitement of the bidding process. This way, the customer can be offered value added services through multiple channels.

Business model and revenue sources

The business models of mobile commerce providers have different success factors than the companies operating in the fixed internet environment. Typically, mobile commerce is characterized by value added services and multichannel strategies combining several medias together. The provider of mobile commerce has to use fixed internet, TV, radio and print media to overcome the limitations in screen size and character input methods. Therefore, some of the early movers are going to be entertainment companies and other content providers which have multiple channels for information provisioning. The mobile terminal can be used as a time-critical and location-independent tool for making a transaction. Because it is personal device, a mobile phone or a PDA is an ideal instrument for payments and other transactions.

In many cases, an internet service provider is acting solely as a gateway to the internet without further intentions. However, mobile internet providers, especially operators, intend to keep all the customers within their mobile portal. This way they are able to generate additional revenue from chargeable value added services. Because they have a billing relationship with the customers, mobile operators are able to offer services with micro-payments. This way, third party developers are also able to offer value added premium services that can be charged on the telephone bill. Naturally, the mobile operator takes a cut of the amount for providing the payment gateway.

Some of the operators have taken a so-called "walled garden" approach towards the mobile internet. This means that the mobile operator does not allow free internet browsing for their customers. In other words, the user cannot enter a particular internet address on her mobile phone and browse information found there. She has to stay within the environment provided by the mobile operator. This way, the operators ensure that the value added services provided by them are actually used. However, consumers accustomed to the fixed internet are not likely to tolerate these kinds of restrictions. It is going to be extremely easy to change the settings of a mobile terminal and start using another service provided by the competitor. Therefore, mobile operators should follow the development closely and respond to consumer action without delay.

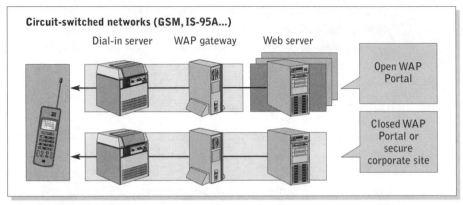

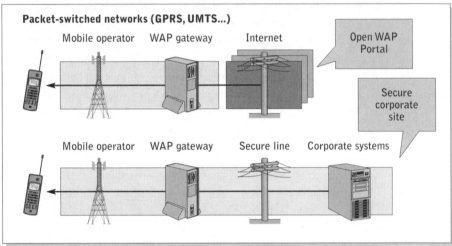

FIGURE 1.18 ■ Users of an open WAP portal are able to access all the WAP sites that are offered through the internet by calling a single number (circuit-switched environment). Closed WAP portal has taken a "walled garden" approach and does not allow free internet browsing. In packet-switched networks, the mobile customer does not make a data call to a specific number. This gives operators stronger control because secure connection to corporate systems has to be acquired via operators. In many cases, secure connections are established with dedicated lines or virtual private networks

As noted earlier, a mobile terminal is not an ideal tool for general browsing on the internet. In contrast, search engines and directories are some of the main applications of the fixed internet and are used for searching global databases and specific documents from all over the world. The fixed internet is characterized by globalization and international content. Mobile internet users are more interested in local information. They want to know what time a movie starts in the theater close by. They want to have access to the local news while on the move. Therefore, the mobile internet will be characterized by local content and information specifically targeted to the user.

The mobile industry is characterized by a fast innovation cycle

The mobile industry is loaded with future expectations and hopes that the emerging technologies will bring new dimensions to existing services. Application developers are looking forward to enhanced terminals with more data processing power and built-in security features. Mobile operators upgrade their networks to offer value added services to the customers. This way, everybody in the mobile internet value chain is affected by the new technology.

The innovation cycle of the fixed internet is very fast. New browsers are introduced regularly and computers and operating systems develop all the time. However, the fixed internet has come to a point where the user does not require the fastest and newest equipment in order to access the services. A computer may be three years old and still the quality of the internet browsing experience is high. This is where we notice the difference between fixed and mobile internet. Can you even imagine trying to browse some of the mobile services with a mobile phone that is three years old? It is simply impossible because the technologies have changed so much.

The innovation cycle of the mobile internet is very fast because of the immature nature of the mobile devices and networks. Developing mobile applications in an environment like this is challenging because the companies have to take into consideration the migration path to the next version. First application providers pay a high price for product development but they also acquire important experience from user requirements and patterns. An early start is essential for those companies wanting to achieve a competitive edge and a critical mass of users before their competitors.

Notes and references

1. Special Report: "Bluetooth Technology Takes off," Wireless International, www.wirelessint.com (August 15, 2000).

2. Brad Smith, "Making Money In M-commerce: Partnering, Platforms And Portals," Wireless Week, www.wirelessweek.com (February 28, 2000).

2

Partnerships

The way to success in the mobile era

While potential markets open up with the emergence of future technology, companies are looking for partners to accomplish the complex mission of service delivery. Basically, three players are positioning themselves in the middle of the value chain: operators, financial institutions and portals. However, they are not likely to succeed without partners. Therefore, the market is characterized by alliances and joint ventures.

The only way to understand market characteristics is to acknowledge the complexity of the value chain and the roles traditional players are taking in order to acquire a position with the maximum revenue potential. Furthermore, zooming into the mobile value chain enables one to see the emerging possibilities and niches caused by the dynamic market structure and totally new business models. New market opportunities exist, not only for established, big players, but for start-up companies as well. Also, the traditional idea of big players having their own game has been shaken as small, innovative companies come up with powerful solutions. Therefore, size is no longer a criteria for cooperation.

The value chain of mobile commerce

The complex structure of the mobile commerce business environment is caused by multiple players, each having different backgrounds and interests.

There are traditional phone operators, internet companies, content providers and completely new, m-commerce start-up companies, each looking for revenue potential and niche markets. However, synergy and cooperation between the parties is an essential part of service delivery because none of the companies are able to create end-to-end solutions alone. Companies are balancing shared interests and individual strategic goals when they are trying to achieve new solutions together. Revenue sharing, customer ownership and transparent cooperation are some of the most critical factors in the mobile commerce value chain. Those companies with the ability to create business-to-business relationships without conflict of interest are the ones most likely to succeed.

With efficient partnership programs, companies are able to acquire skills and expertise outside their core competence. However, some of the early movers have taken a different approach and developed these skills within the company. Finnish operator, Sonera, for example, has developed SmartTrust, a mobile payment and security solution so it will be the first on the market. This way, Sonera is able to control a wider spectrum of the value chain. As it is one of the basic components in payment and security, SmartTrust can be used all over the world in various mobile commerce solutions. With SmartTrust, Sonera is expanding to cover international activity instead of acting in a small domestic market. SmartTrust can be used by portal providers and financial institutions to reduce the time to market because organizations without security skills are able to partner Sonera and concentrate on their core competencies.

The dynamic structure of the emerging market presents threats to several traditional companies. While the value chain of mobile commerce is in the middle of great changes, companies are aggressively searching for new opportunities for expansion, their competitors and other players in the field. For example, portal sites of mobile operators could be replaced by strong content providers or virtual operators. Additionally, network-based security solutions might suffer significant revenue loss if devices had security built in. Financial institutions are also in danger of losing some of their customers if mobile operators apply for banking licenses, offering bank accounts and convenient micro-payments to visitors of their mobile sites. In contrast, some of the banks are already building their own mobile portals, offering payment services to third party merchants selling products online. This way, the banks are able to retain a direct customer relationship in a highly competitive environment.

FIGURE 2.1 ■ The web page of SmartTrust

Most mobile commerce players want a direct customer relationship and a strong brand. This is natural as companies secure their position from being disintermediated or replaced. Therefore, partnerships should be based on common goals and clearly defined objectives. Organizations are looking for partnerships not only to fill the gaps in their core competencies, but also for greater control of the current position. Swedish operator, Telia, is working with Volvo to offer value added services for future cars. By doing this, Telia will have greater control of the value chain when the new services become commercially available. It can also use the acquired knowledge for building similar solutions internationally. As the margin of the voice traffic decreases, Telia has to be prepared not to be disintermediated from the new, promising market of advanced data services.

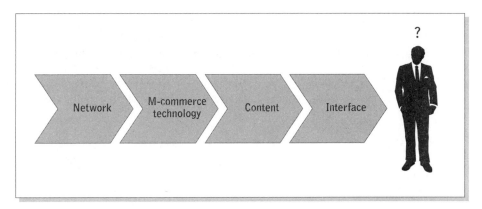

FIGURE 2.2 ■ The four main components in the mobile commerce value chain

Basically, there are four main components in the value chain. These are network, m-commerce technology, content and interface. These four components include sub-components that will be discussed later in this chapter. The beginning of the value chain is characterized by business-to-business opportunities because the basic technologies are needed in all mobile commerce projects. For example, servers and security applications are some of the basic components of every mobile commerce solution. In the eyes of a consumer, the companies providing the basic services seldom have a strong brand or direct customer relationship

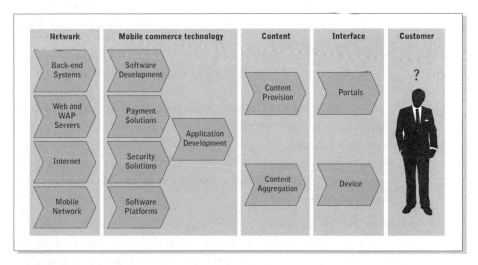

FIGURE 2.3 ■ A detailed mobile commerce value chain

with the end user because they operate in a business-to-business environment. However, direct customer relationships and a strong consumer brand become increasingly important when moving toward the end of the value chain.

Let's look at the value chain in detail to address business opportunities and understand the strategic intentions of different players.

Network

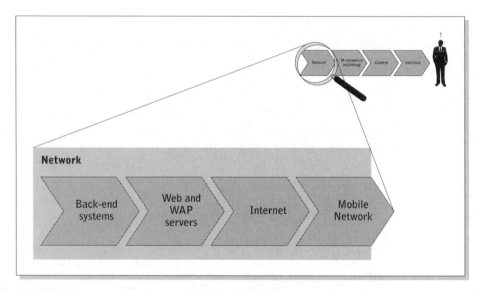

FIGURE 2.4   ■   Network includes four sub-components

Network is a fundamental part of the value chain because it prepares the foundation for value added services and transactions. The basic components of network are back-end systems, web and WAP servers, internet and mobile networks. Although all the components are not literally network related, it is a good common denominator for everything that can be found from the beginning of the value chain.

Most of the components are evident for those familiar with e-commerce. Corporate back-end systems, provided by companies such as SAP, Oracle, Siebel and i2 lay the foundation for real-time, net-centric architecture. Many e-commerce or m-commerce applications require back-end system integration to enable advanced features. Massive amounts of data are stored and accessed in customer relationship management, enterprise resource planning and supply chain management software. For example, the struggle over customer ownership comes down to billing systems and customer relationship management software, where the actual data is stored. The owner of these databases is able to perform precisely targeted marketing and save money by knowing the personal profiles of customers.

With net-centric architecture, back-end systems are tied to web and WAP servers. Systems integrators are needed to build custom pieces of software which respond to requests from a mobile terminal. Actually, systems integrators are also needed in numerous other instances along the mobile commerce value chain because they wrap individual applications and solutions together into one value added service. Also, companies with strong e-commerce capabilities are well positioned regarding mobile commerce because their network infrastructure and software architecture to deliver the services is substantially better than others who are just exploring the possibilities of e-commerce. Also, similarity in market strategies and the fast development cycle of e-commerce have better prepared the organizations to address mobile customers.

With the emergence of Wireless Application Protocol (WAP), several business opportunities have opened up for software developers. New start-up companies are developing WAP servers and back-end system providers, such as SAP and Siebel, offer mobile extensions for their existing products. Openwave (formerly known as Phone.com) has taken an aggressive approach to acquire greater control of the value chain. They offer a free micro-browser with Openwave-specific features to phone manufacturers and charge mobile operators using their WAP gateway. This way, Openwave is able to control both ends of the value chain and ensure the functionality of WAP services developed for their micro-browsers and gateways. In addition, Openwave offers a portal platform for operators integrating various applications into one package.

Openwave is naturally not able to have a direct customer relationship or a strong brand among consumers but it is positioned well regarding corporate customers. By having a Openwave micro-browser in a massive number of terminals, the company's WAP gateway and portal platform are natural selections for mobile operators offering services in markets with high Openwave micro-browser penetration. Additionally, mobile device manufacturers without the skills to develop a micro-browser of their own can reduce their time to market when using the free product provided by Openwave.

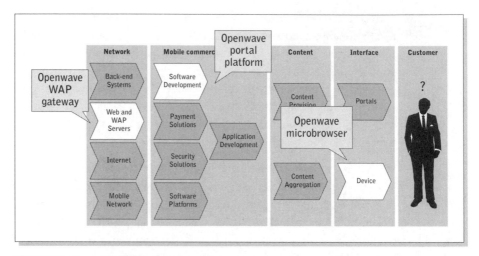

FIGURE 2.5 ■ Openwave has been able to provide products that complement each other at both ends of the value chain

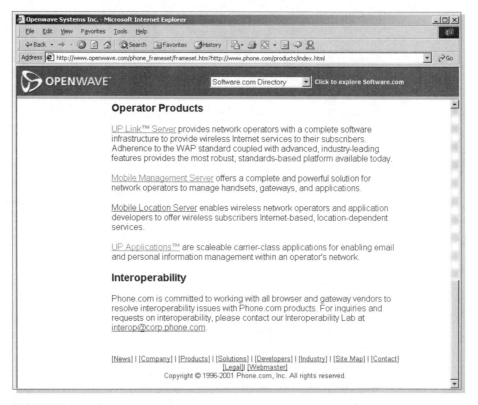

FIGURE 2.6 ■ Openwave products

Internet service providers (ISPs) offer internet connections to deliver information from back-end systems to the mobile network. The service may be provided by traditional phone operators or ISPs renting bandwidth from the operators. In the e-commerce world, ISPs have tried to acquire a stronger position in the value chain by establishing portals and other value added services. America Online is one of the successful internet service providers that has been able to create customer loyalty by offering extra services. Now, with the emergence of mobile commerce, ISPs are looking for partnerships in order to strengthen their position. America Online, for example, is developing mobile services in cooperation with General Motors.

The mobile network is the next component in the value chain. It receives the information from the internet and provides a direct connection to a mobile device. Because it has the lowest and most expensive bandwidth, the mobile network sets the limits for many other components in the value chain. Application developers need to optimize mobile solutions for data transmission rates between a mobile network and the terminal of the end user. Mobile networks also affect the development of terminals. Concurrently, with a roll out of the sophisticated network technologies, new, high-end smart terminals are entering the market with integrated e-mail, voice, video and calendar software. Smart terminals are able to take full advantage of the modern network technology.

M-commerce technology

Mobile commerce technology is full of opportunities. Systems integrators cooperate with portal providers to create scalable, industry strength mobile portal platforms. Dotcom companies innovate payment and security solutions. Microsoft and Symbian compete to generate cutting-edge operating systems for future terminals. Application developers package all the components into one, value added service. Without a doubt, m-commerce technology is one of the most promising fields in the value chain. Early movers are able to generate substantial profits with their software and lead the markets in the direction they desire. In contrast, there is a danger of becoming overtaken by the other early movers. Big, established financial institutions might run over innovative start-ups in payment solutions. Application developers are in danger of isolation without strategic partnerships. Network-based security solutions might be replaced with open source solutions from device manufacturers. To sum up: big profits do not come without risk in this area.

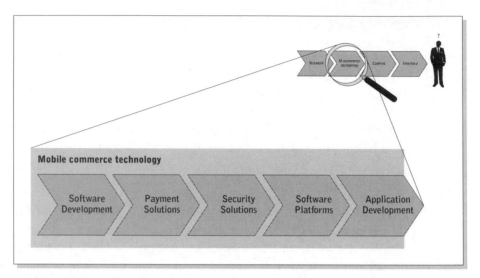

FIGURE 2.7 ▪ M-commerce technology is a sub-component of the mobile commerce value chain

Software development takes place by providing the other intermediaries with basic platforms. Mobile portals integrating e-mail, calendar and news are examples of such solutions. Software developers aim to produce an architecture where new applications can be easily attached to the variety of old ones within a short period of time. This reduces the time to market and enables portal providers to offer new services with shorter development cycles. Also, the old applications can be updated faster because the common framework is already in place.

Payment solutions is another interesting area in mobile commerce technology. Mobile operators have a direct billing relationship with the customer, so they are in a key position to offer transaction services for third party merchants. Micropayments can easily be billed on the telephone. On the other hand, operators may feel uncomfortable with the risk of bad debt, especially if they are charging for third parties. Therefore, banks and operators are likely to form joint ventures to offer payment solutions for their customers.

In the long run, financial institutions are in danger of being removed from the value chain by mobile operators. The race over customer ownership currently favors mobile operators who retain a billing relationship with their customers. Therefore, banks should seek partnerships where customer information can be shared and the brand recognition of the partners would be equal. A Scandinavian bank, Nordea, has already acted against disintermediation. They have a financial portal with third party merchants who benefit from Nordea's direct transaction capabilities and a massive number of regular visitors. The customers may visit Nordea's portal regardless of their mobile operator because Nordea has an internal WAP gateway. Therefore, customers are not relying on a certain operator as would be the case if they were positioned with an operator's portal market place. Customer security can also be provided because the WAP gateway resides within the financial institution. However, it remains to be seen if financial institutions are able to provide customers with such a variety of services that they can compete with the portals of mobile operators and content providers.

Security solutions are an integral part of online transactions. E-commerce security leaks have already proven that security is a vulnerable area. Companies with established brands are always in danger of losing some of their customers if there are public security problems with electronic or mobile commerce.

Security is needed in order to ensure:

➤ confidentiality for the parties involved in a transaction;

➤ authentication of buyer and seller;

➤ authorization of the transaction;

➤ integrity of data;

➤ non-repudiation of a transaction.

Partnerships are needed in this area in order to provide companies with a deeper understanding of security and to share the risks involved in commercial ventures. Security providers often cooperate with transaction providers to make commercial products which combine both online payments and security.

With the emerging mobile commerce, there are substantial opportunities for security software. However, the dynamic structure of the market presents threats to these players as well. Device manufacturers want to make mobile terminal wallets that could be used for both e-commerce and m-commerce transactions. In contrast, mobile operators in favor of network-based solutions are trying to take the market in a direction where operators are the trusted third parties, capable of issuing certificates to customers.

Another area of competition in the value chain is software platforms for future terminals. Mobile devices are a lucrative market for operating system developers. Development takes place in partnerships where each of the partners bring their core competencies to the table. One wrong move in the operating system race may cost device manufacturers a fortune.

Microsoft is developing Pocket PC for PDA devices and smart phone platform called Smartphone 2002 for future terminals. Obviously, Pocket PC and Smartphone 2002 will benefit from the success of the other Microsoft operating systems because they are compatible with Windows. It is easy for application developers to make programs on a platform they already know. The other player in the market is an industry consortium of the mobile handset manufacturers: Symbian. Symbian is developing Symbian OS, the operating system initially developed by UK-based PDA manufacturer Psion. 3Com, the developer of Palm OS, is partnering with Psion and Nokia to develop a common standard.

Application developers should pay close attention to the mobile operating system war. Partnerships with industry leaders may offer valuable first hand information to help application developers focus on the right solutions. It is also in the interest of platform developers to create an environment where application development tools are easily accessible. One of the strengths of Microsoft has always been superb development tools.

Application developers are the final link in mobile commerce technology. Initially, they concentrated on Windows CE, PalmOS and Symbian OS32 platforms. The applications traditionally presented offline content with the ability to synchronize information from the internet. However, the emergence of WAP and packet-switched mobile networks has led the development from platform-centric to net-centric, where the application resides on servers hosted by operators, ISPs or corporations. Therefore, real-time applications with online connection to back-end systems can now be created.

Application developers hold a prominent position in the mobile commerce value chain. In some cases, they are systems integrators who package back-end systems, payment and security solutions into one service. Sometimes, they are internet start-up companies doing a spin-off to mobile commerce. Partnerships with other intermediaries are needed to take full advantage of the promising market. Internet companies should seek partnerships and the expertise of systems integrators to be able to acquire larger deals. Membership in industry consortiums such as WAP Forum might help application developers attain a competitive edge. This way, they are able to predict the future and even participate in making it.

Content

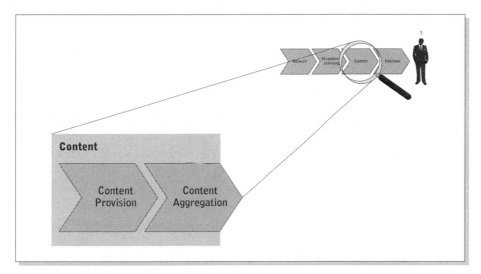

FIGURE 2.8 ■ Content provision and aggregation are a part of the mobile commerce value chain

Content is a key factor in making a mobile service that attracts users and keeps them coming back. E-commerce has already shown how valuable customers regard the right content. The users of America Online spend 80% of their time within the AOL service. What does this mean to AOL? America Online is able to benefit from the loyalty of their customers and generate more advertising revenue. Also, AOL can track the habits of their customers and develop the service further.

However, the mobile environment is different in nature. The models of electronic commerce can not be imported directly. There are several reasons for this. First, a mobile device has a limited form factory compared to the devices used for internet browsing. Typing text is always more difficult. Therefore, services that require a lot of writing are not suitable for the mobile environment. In contrast, a service where users select options from a list is more likely to succeed. In addition to the limited text pad, the screen of a mobile device is substantially smaller than the one in computers. This sets limits for graphics and the amount of text. Second, a mobile device is more personal than the computers used for internet browsing. Often, many people use the same computer to browse the internet. A mobile phone is used by just one person, or at most, a family. Because of the personal nature of a mobile device and the limited form factory, content personalization is more important in the mobile world. Third, mobile phones are used mostly when moving from one point to another. Therefore, the importance of location-based services will increase. Also, location-based services, together with personalization, enable full use of the limited text pad and small screen size.

Traditional content providers are engaging in partnerships with numerous intermediaries of the mobile commerce value chain to benefit from the promising market. Reuters delivers news information together with Ericsson and Nokia. In addition, it has teamed up with existing internet portals like Yahoo! and Excite to provide information for their mobile portals. Recognizing the possibilities of mobile markets, Reuters is also building their own mobile portals around the world, which ensures its visibility in the future and maximizes its presence in the value chain.

As mobile terminal penetration increases, competition in mobile services will be even tougher than today and those who survive are companies that are able to provide exciting and convenient services to consumers. Therefore, content providers are looking for ways to process information using modern technologies such as personalization and location. The small screen size and the limited text insertion capabilities will increase the importance of convenient content services with less browsing and fewer options to choose.

Content providers should seek partnerships with content aggregators, gathering information from various sources. Small content providers in particular are vulnerable without strong partners. Therefore, a partnership with a content aggregator such as a mobile portal helps in acquiring higher visibility in the market and regular revenue. However, it is crucial for a content provider to differentiate its service from the mass of other content providers. If there is a market situation where ten sports information companies are offering the same services, the first to drop out is the one without any extras. Without partnerships and differentiation, content providers are in danger of being disintermediated from the value chain of mobile commerce.

There are two ways to process information in order to create differentiated services: technical differentiation and human expertise. Human expertise is needed in creating interesting stories and describing the people behind them.

It is something that only those with the ability to write creatively are able to do. In contrast, technical differentiation uses software tools and custom solutions in order to process information. For example, during the era of mobile commerce, content providers are able to use personalization, location technology and instant messaging for technical differentiation.

Content aggregators gather information from various sources and offer content providers a channel on which to market their information. Depending on a business model, content aggregators may purchase information from third parties or develop services in joint ventures with them. Mobile operators, web portals and financial institutions may act as content aggregators, providing their mobile customers with a variety of applications. The main reason for content is always to attract customers to visit the site regularly. Therefore, portal companies are looking for ways to attract as many consumers as possible with customer segmentation. Different age groups and mobile device user segments have variable needs and expectations regarding content. All of those needs should be nurtured in order to attract regular visitors. They increase the revenue generated from increased airtime and are possibly suitable targets for mobile advertising. Additionally, interesting services and regular visitors are the only way for long term profitability and securing a position in the value chain of the future.

Whether they are mobile operators, web portals or advertisers, content aggregators should be able to personalize content and optimize it for the needs of individuals. Partnerships with systems integrators and application developers help content aggregators in creating personalized content. They are able to set up content management software and create appropriate guidelines for using it. Additionally, systems integrators can help the company integrate billing systems, customer relationship management software and other corporate systems into the service.

Another way to process content is to attach location coordinates to it. That way content becomes local and the user can access local services more easily. Who needs to know what time movies start in Washington D.C. if they live in New York? Using a localized mobile portal, the user does not have to search for the closest movie theaters. They are displayed automatically. Mobile operators are in a prominent position because they are capable of determining the location of an individual handset. Therefore, partnerships with them are needed in order to create location-based services. Mobile operators are also in a position where they can pre-configure the telephones to contact their portals directly without further settings. This will be a remarkable advantage for operators to market their own portals. Content aggregators partnering with these portals are able to benefit from a wide subscriber base and regular visitors.

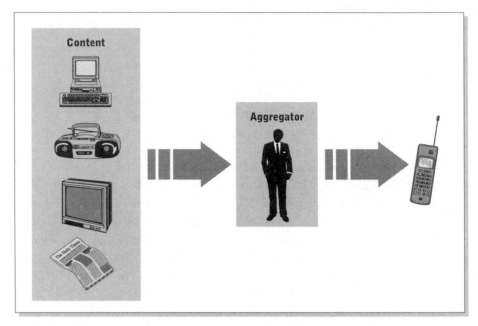

FIGURE 2.9 ■ Content aggregators collect information and services and repackage them to be offered to mobile users

Interface

Interface is the component in the value chain in which customer ownership and brand awareness are the key points in terms of success and revenue. Traditionally, both financial institutions and mobile operators have been able to retain a direct customer relationship with the consumer. Banks manage their accounts and handle a series of other services related to finance. Mobile operators have a direct billing relationship with the consumer. In addition, they provide consumers with identifiable handsets. This enables them to pre-configure the phones and set their desired start page.

Today, the value chain is changing and the roles of the players are in turmoil. Financial institutions are developing mobile portals in order to secure their place in the future value chain. Content providers and aggregators are establishing portals with personal communication services to acquire more visibility in the market. Mobile operators develop portals as well. Some of them are moving in a direction where they will become providers of financial services. In other words, everybody wants to secure their place in the value chain. Furthermore, the players are looking for partnerships where they are able to provide a single place for consumers to handle their everyday routines.

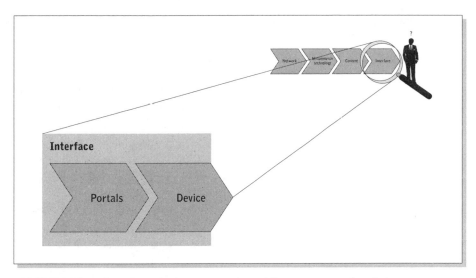

FIGURE 2.10 ■ Interface: the last stop on the mobile commerce value chain

There are several reasons for a bank to enter into mobile commerce. First, by educating customers to handle their finances online, banks are able to acquire substantial cost savings with reduced transaction and fixed costs. The number of "bricks and mortar" branches can be reduced while the same level of customer service is offered. Second, competition from both outside and inside the industry compels banks to look for innovative channels and models for more customer-oriented service. Third, the emerging mobile commerce will enable banks to participate in revenue sharing and offers new opportunities to act as a trusted third party in transactions. In addition, banks are able to use their payment and service infrastructure by offering payment services for those engaged in mobile commerce. This way, banks deliver the security and authentication services for parties involved in a transaction.

Looking for synergy and distribution channel

Portugal Telecom, Banco Espirito Santo (BES) and Portuguese state bank Caixa Geral de Depósitos (CGD) formed a strategic alliance in order to provide business-to-business, business-to-consumer and mobile commerce services together. The companies seek synergy by drawing on a combined client base of 8.7 million people. Under the agreement, Portugal Telecom takes a 3 per cent stake in BES and BES increased its stake in Portugal Telecom to 6 per cent.

Portugal Telecom is also participating in CAIXANET, a new company owned jointly by CGD and Portugal Telecom though its subsidiaries. The goal of CAIXANET is to conceive, develop, manage and explore new distribution channels for CGD.

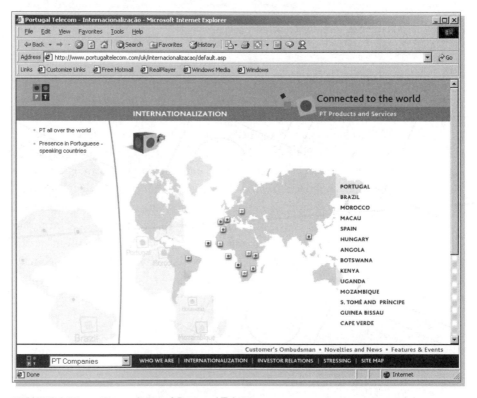

FIGURE 2.11 ■ The website of Portugal Telecom

Stock brokerages should enter the mobile commerce environment to provide better service for customers. A mobile device would be an ideal tool for a day trader who needs to be constantly aware of the market situation. Ubiquity of the mobile device opens up a whole new behavior, where people subscribe to personalized alert services to keep up with the markets. If I had invested in Nokia, I would surely be grateful to know, in real time, when the stock price goes up or down to a certain level.

Portal sites are offered in order to attract the customer by providing a "one-stop" location for various services. A portal may include e-mail, calendar and banking services, together with personalized news and community pages. Portals play an important role in the interface component of the value chain because the provider of a portal usually has a direct customer relationship with the user.

There are four players that are likely to offer mobile portal services:

- ➤ mobile operators;
- ➤ financial institutions;
- ➤ web portals and internet service providers;
- ➤ strong content brands.

At the initial stage of mobile commerce, portal services are charged according to online time. Agreements with mobile operators are necessary in order to share the revenue from increased call charges. Later on, with the emergence of packet switched data, services will be charged based on transmitted data. In either case, the mobile operator is likely to generate revenue by providing a physical network. However, over time, the margin of pure transmittance services is dropping and the competition is increasing. Therefore, operators are establishing portal services to generate extra income from the value added content.

Mobile portal providers should focus on the distribution channel of their service. With the exception of mobile operators, the others are in danger of being isolated without efficient partnerships which provide a distribution channel for their services. Device manufacturers may offer a distribution channel to portals by inserting the settings of the portal readily in the micro-browser. This way, the customer may access the portal as soon as he gets the phone without additional configuration. The operator portals face increasing competition, because they are not the only ones providing default portal access. The only income a mobile operator is able to generate if a consumer uses an external portal is a low margin network connection because it acts solely as a "bit pipe".

Handset manufacturers and vendors are the last stop in the value chain. Consumers are looking for a phone brand rather than a particular mobile operator or service provider. A mobile phone is a very personal device. Manufacturers are, therefore, making a wide variety of devices to satisfy different customer needs. Consumers have shown a clear tendency toward even more personalized devices – customized ringing tones and logos are popular applications for mobile portal providers. Replaceable covers with different shapes and colors have also been successful.

The largest mobile phone manufacturers, Nokia, Ericsson and Motorola, are also strong in mobile network infrastructure. Therefore, they have a head start in bringing new terminals to the market that support GPRS and UMTS. On the other hand, device manufacturers are likely to be the bottleneck for new technologies. With WAP, for example, manufacturers could not bring the new terminals to the market within the promised time frame. Many portals were open before WAP phones entered the market.

Device manufacturers affect the new services provided by the portals. So far, Nokia and Ericsson have pushed WAP development heavily by partnering with system integrators and service providers to bring new, innovative solutions to the market. Additionally, both have a venture organization that supports and invests in promising start-up companies that use the new technologies. In the future, device manufacturers are likely to drive the adoption of multimedia messaging, streaming video, music and network games using GPRS and UMTS. This way, the technology they have developed can be presented to consumers in a convenient manner.

Content providers and system integrators should seek partnerships with device manufacturers and vendors because they are able to benefit from common interests and leverage each others' knowledge. Additionally, the parties seldom have conflicts of interest because their tasks in the value chain are distinct.

3

Consumer mobile commerce

Mass market solutions with segmentation

What would you buy using a mobile phone?

Would you buy a stereo, gifts, food or clothes using your mobile phone? I doubt it. What about music, tickets, stocks or ringing tones? Maybe. Well, would you be happy to receive a notification on your phone if your favorite artist was in town? In most cases, yes, depending on who's paying.

The key questions to ask in planning mobile commerce solutions are:

➤ Would it be easier to purchase this item by any other means?

➤ Do I get anything extra when using my mobile phone for this purchase?

➤ Can I receive enough information on the product this way?

Most products currently sold over the fixed internet are not suitable for mobile commerce. The limitations in screen size and text input make it very hard to use a mobile device, whether it is a phone or a PDA, for internet browsing. Therefore, mobile commerce will be something completely different from traditional e-commerce.

Mobile and fixed internet

The hype surrounding consumer mobile commerce is logical. It is a natural extension of electronic commerce which casts the internet even wider than today. Mobile commerce is about extending the reach of the existing fixed internet applications to cover those people that do not necessarily bother to learn to use "complicated" PCs. However, mobile commerce applications are able to offer the biggest value when they are combined with existing media, such as the fixed internet, television or radio. This way, the limitations of mobile terminals and networks can be overcome at the same time as the obvious advantages of ubiquity and instant connectivity which are used to offer value added services.

Mobile internet is important because it provides some fixed internet services to people without PCs. The price of mobile terminals is very competitive compared to computers, so they are likely to become increasingly important over time. People who use PCs just to access their e-mail may shift to using mobile devices for convenience and instant connectivity. Those who do not have any experience with computers can easily learn to use mobile phones; there is no software installation or modem configuration needed. In western countries, nearly everybody has a TV and radio. The penetration of mobile devices is likely to increase to 70-80 per cent in most of these countries. Therefore, we will see exciting solutions when mass market mobile and broadcasting are brought together.

Most of the e-commerce software architecture and network infrastructure can be used to provide mobile services. Therefore, dotcom companies have a better chance to succeed if they are able to partner with content providers and the existing media. Business models of mobile commerce may well be a combination of old and new. Already-buried push applications of e-commerce will see the light again as messages can be sent directly to mobile terminals. This way, time sensitive alert messages are used to provide value added services. Another trend, personalization, will face increasing demands because the limited screens make internet surfing inconvenient. Information has to be right there. To sum up, the difference between mobile and fixed internet commerce is in user behavior. Mobile users are likely to prefer push solutions. Others are satisfied with pull applications such as fixed internet surfing.

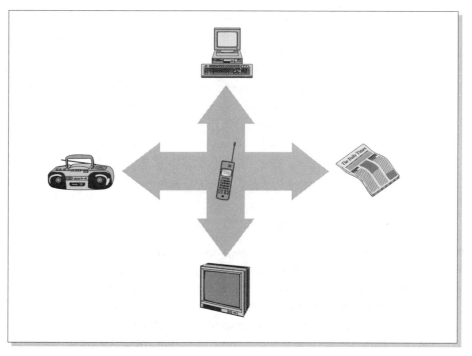

FIGURE 3.1 ▦ Multi-channel strategies combine the fixed internet, print, television and radio in order to create service concepts

Characteristics of a mobile device

In order to understand the user requirements in mobile commerce, it is helpful to take a better look at the specific characteristics of a mobile device.

Convenience and instant connectivity

A mobile phone or a PDA is a convenient way to handle various personal tasks. With an internet-capable device, a person is able to use calendar, e-mail, banking and entertainment services together with traditional voice calls. Also, mobile phones are typically easier to use than computers. Operating systems are integrated into the device so there is no software installation needed when buying a new phone or a PDA. The user does not need any previous knowledge of the particular device or software. Convenience is the major factor, causing the rapid explosion of mobile markets.

Mobile devices are also characterized by zero boot time. You don't have to wait until the operating system is up and running as is the case with computers. This enables mobile devices to be used spontaneously without frustrating delays. With the introduction of packet-switched services like GPRS, a mobile phone can connect to the internet instantly. In practice, when you see an advertisement on television, you will be able to take your mobile device and receive additional information by going to the advertised web page. Because of instant connection, advertisers are likely to use multichannel strategies, where TV or radio is used for broadcasting and mobile devices are used for ordering and additional information.

Intimacy of a mobile device

Mobile phones are very personal devices. The success of customized ringing tones and logos shows how individuals want to personalize their mobile phones. The personal characteristics of a mobile phone can be used to facilitate the limited form factor of the devices. Default information can be inserted into the memory of the device and retrieved from there when purchasing online. This alleviates the filling of complex order forms and hastens the time to make an online purchase.

The personal manner of the mobile phone enables secure certificates to be stored inside the device. Security of mobile commerce can thus be developed to address current concerns, where consumers are afraid to purchase online. In countries with high mobile phone penetration, mobile devices could be used to secure e-commerce as well. For example, SmartTrust can be used to secure online stock trading when using a fixed internet connection. Secure transactions with strong PKI encryption can be done using a special SIM card inserted into the mobile phone.

Anywhere, anytime

Yet another characteristic of mobile devices is independence of location or time. In order to use a mobile phone for shopping, you do not have to be in a certain place at a certain time. Ubiquity of the mobile device is interactive in nature. I can connect to any service, regardless of my position. On the other hand, I can receive information anywhere because the terminal is always with me. The latter enables services where a consumer is able to receive personalized alert messages when something important is happening to him or to his family. "*Your loan has been approved!*" "*You've got mail!*" "*Your favorite TV show starts!*" "*You have not paid the electricity bill!*" These are just some of the services that are able to be offered in a personalized environment where the receiver of the message is always available.

Location-based services have great potential to become killer applications of the mobile environment. This is because awareness of location is one of the basic interactivity components. "Where are you?" This question has been asked millions of times when communicating via mobile devices. Now, the network is able to define your geographical position and this information can be used when offering products or services for your needs. "*I have a car breakdown in the middle of nowhere, send me a tow truck!*" "*There is a traffic jam five kilometers ahead, use the alternative highway!*" "*Your son is on Addison Square, should you meet there?*" "*There has been a nuclear accident in your area, please wait for further instructions!*" These kind of services are possible with location technology.

Mobile commerce applications

Shopping

The usage patterns of fixed internet electronic commerce and mobile commerce are fundamentally different. While most fixed internet users surf the web for a long time, reading product specifications and looking at pictures of the items, mobile terminals are used for impulse buying when additional information is not needed. The optimal goal of mobile manufacturers must, therefore, be one-click transactions without lengthy forms or additional procedures. This leaves the stores with two possible directions: either the items have to be very simple, or there must be an additional channel for providing information.

Retailing

Mobile retailing business models are completely different from the fixed internet. A company simply cannot place an entire shopping catalog into the mobile environment. The limitations in screen size and character input make it impossible to browse all the categories and select the products you like. The user interface is subject to multiple challenges. First, the shopping process has to be fast, taking a couple of minutes from the beginning to the end. Second, there cannot be long forms to fill in, otherwise the process becomes too slow and cumbersome. Third, reading long descriptions about products using a mobile terminal is very clumsy, so the name of the product must include most of the information the buyer needs. So, should we just forget mobile retailing and move on to some other topics? Let's give it a try and see how the described challenges can be overcome.

To begin with, there has to be a central system that includes a user profile for the consumer. This profile stores bank details, address and everything else relevant to all the shopping transactions made using the mobile terminal. There are three possibilities. The required information can be stored into the smart card inside the mobile terminal, mobile operator's network or a system provided by third parties. The ultimate goal is that the same information can be used regardless of the manufacturer. Right now, a widespread solution for personal information provisioning does not exist. The only way to automate the shopping process in the short term is to encourage users to personalize the service using a fixed internet interface. Personalization removes two of the initial problems by making the shopping process faster and eliminating forms. The third problem, user interface, has to be considered when deciding what kind of products are actually suitable for mobile commerce.

CASE STUDY

Trintech PayWare

Trintech's PayWare enables mobile customers to store their payment, contact and delivery details on a secure server instead of having to enter all that information on a phone keypad every time they make a purchase. WAP phone users are able to complete transactions by calling up their details by following a link on the retailer's WAP service and entering a PIN code. Therefore, the retailer has to have an agreement with Trintech in order to make the service possible. Trintech has agreements with a credit card company, Visa International, and WAP product seller, Openwave.

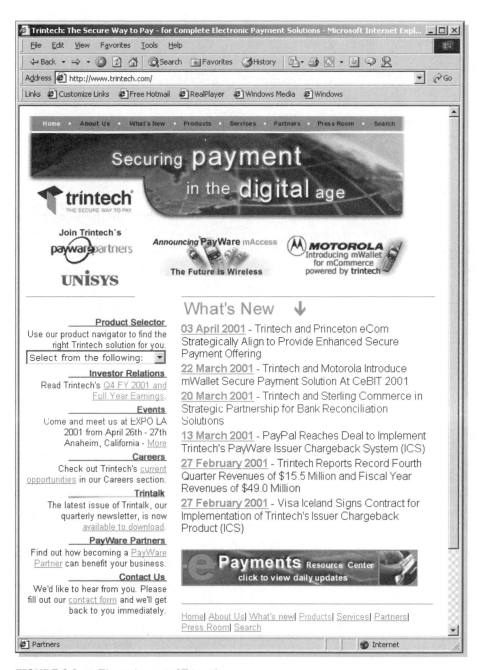

FIGURE 3.2 ■ The web page of Trintech

On top of the user interface challenges, other hot topics of mobile retailing should be considered. Why would the consumer want to use a mobile device instead of a PC or some other means? What makes the product so desirable that the person cannot wait to use more convenient ordering channels? Multichannel strategies combining television, radio and print media, together with a mobile channel, make it easy to order products instantly. This way, the media without natural interaction is able to use the ubiquity of mobile devices in order to create a channel for feedback. Therefore, the media surrounding us wherever we go and a mobile device, always by our side, forms a strategic alliance to offer retail goods regardless of our location.

Another emerging use of mobile terminals is comparison shopping. Using a mobile device, a shopper is able to access comparison shopping services for reviewing prices and specifications of other, similar products. This way, she can make more informed decisions and negotiate lower prices. It is likely that intelligent agents will emerge with comparison shopping services. The introduction of packet-switched networks will make the use of comparison shopping services more convenient because devices are able to connect to the internet instantly.

▪▪ CASE STUDY

Scan

Scan has launched a service which enables shoppers to check whether items they intend to purchase in the real world are cheaper online. The user sends the ISBN number of a book or a barcode on a CD as a text message to UK-based Scan. In return, Scan checks online retailers such as Amazon.com and Jungle to see how much they are asking for the same product and send prices back via instant messaging. The user is able to purchase items sold online directly by responding to a text message. Barcodes and ISBN numbers are standardized across Europe, so they can be used to check the prices of other merchants.

▪▪ CASE STUDY

Edmunds.com

A company from Santa Monica, California offers an online comparison shopping service for car buyers. They are able to check prices and model configurations using mobile phones or PDAs. In order to enable convenient use regardless of mobile terminal of the user, Edmunds.com has created a pair of sites.

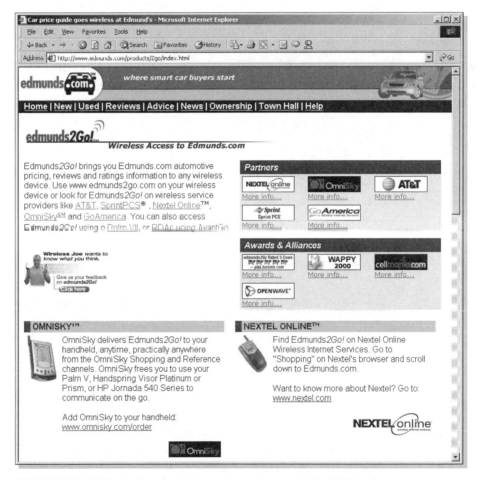

FIGURE 3.3 ▪ Edmunds.com can be accessed using a variety of different devices

Auctions

Auctioning is one of the most successful business models of the fixed internet. Both consumers and businesses use auction services, partly because of the excitement, partly because of convenience and the ability to find bargains. The bidding process of auctions becomes faster and more intense as the time draws to an end. Auctioning is actually very time sensitive, requiring immediate action as the bids of the other participants enter into the system. Another feature favorable to mobile terminals is the short length of the messages that are transferred between the system and the user. The only information needed to respond to the auction system is the name of the product, highest bid at the moment, closing time and amount of the smallest possible raise. Therefore, the process of an auction can be easily integrated into the mobile environment.

Because of the time sensitive nature of an auction process, the bearer of the message has to be reliable and close to real-time connection. SMS messages are not the best way to build a real-time auction service because there can be delays in message transportation. Therefore, a new form of instant messaging, USSD, is better suited for mobile auctions because it provides a real-time connection between the service provider and a mobile terminal. Using USSD, a session stays open until the user disconnects it. The messages can have up to 182 characters and the service is best suited for transactions that need instant confirmation. Packet-switched networks will make mobile auctions easier in the future because the session is open all the time and the cost to the user is generated only when data is transmitted.

Mobile auctions are likely to follow the same pattern of multichannel approach as retailing and many other services in the m-commerce space. The fixed internet is used to configure the service and type in all the information needed to deliver the products. After that, time critical content is pushed to a mobile terminal and it can be used to close the deal.

Ticketing and reservations

Mobile ticketing was one of the first applications to enter the m-commerce market for internet-capable devices. Ticketing has a strong potential for the mobile environment, because the purchasing process is straightforward and requires only a small amount of information to be transferred. Therefore, the limited user interface of mobile devices is suitable for the process. Additionally, ticketing consists of small cost items that are, in many cases, based on impulse buying. The decision to go to movies or concerts can, therefore, be made while on the move with friends and family.

12Snap, Germany

12Snap is a shopping and auction portal providing the customers with tools and applications to conduct time critical transactions using their mobile phones. Using the fixed internet, consumers are able to enter their personal details and preferences while selecting items of their interest. The company has deployed a cell broadcast service to notify the customers of auctions. Short messages are used to inform the users when their bid has been exceeded. This way they are always aware of the bidding process without having to access a website regularly. The final step, payment, is done by speaking to a call center representative.

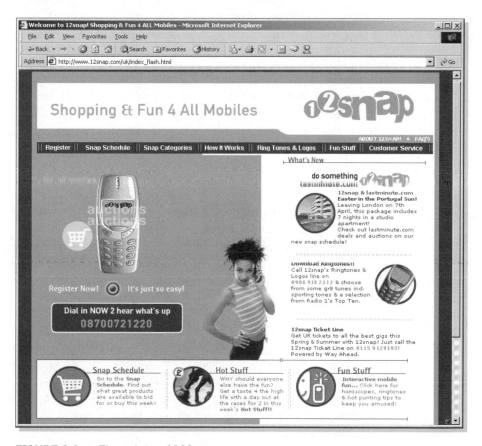

FIGURE 3.4 ■ The website of 12Snap

Companies offering mobile ticketing have many different approaches towards the actual ticket delivery. Simple solutions offer reservations for traditional tickets that have to be paid when entering a movie theater or a concert hall. After making the reservation, the user gets a reservation number that must be remembered when paying for the tickets at the counter. This solution requires some back-end system integration because availability of the tickets must be checked during the user session. Additionally, location of the seats should be optimized dynamically because that information is a crucial point in making a decision about a particular show.

The next level of mobile ticketing is to immediately pay for the tickets online. This can be done with a mobile bank transfer or operator's charging account. In case of charging, the mobile operator has a separate system for charging small-ticket purchases with a telephone bill. This way, the operator offers charging services for third parties conducting mobile business. The paid tickets can be acquired by showing the reservation number at the counter.

The most advanced level of mobile ticket delivery consists of electronic tickets stored into the smart card or memory of the mobile terminal. The arrival of Bluetooth technology enables the electronic tickets to be checked automatically at the entrance. Another way is to send a reservation number to a mobile phone via SMS messaging. That number is reviewed when entering the theatre. In this case, the ticket collectors standing at the entrance should have terminals connected to the central system.

System integration is one of the most important issues when designing an effective ticketing system. Some movie theaters already have systems enabling online ticketing using the fixed internet interface. These companies are best equipped to offer mobile ticketing because their back-end systems are connected to the internet with a real-time link. However, the mobile environment enables completely new service concepts to be created as well.

Push and personalization technology become increasingly important when designing the new mobile systems. For example, using a PC, the consumer is able to check forthcoming movies. When the time of the premiere is at hand, a short message is received on the mobile terminal, suggesting that it is time to book the tickets for the movie selected earlier. This is an excellent way to build customer loyalty and provide value added services adapted to the mobile environment.

Ticketmaster

Ticketmaster is one of the leading e-commerce portals offering sports, concert, theater and many other tickets via a fixed internet interface. The wireless service, called Local Intelligence, is available in 32 metropolitan areas offering a WAP and a short messaging interface to a variety of mobile terminals. Initially, users were able to purchase tickets for several events available at the Ticketmaster website. Later on, more advanced functions such as personalized profiles and reminders were introduced. The revenue is generated from ticket surcharges, sponsorships and advertising.

FIGURE 3.5 ■ Ticketmaster Online Citysearch offers a mobile extension for the existing web services

Movie tickets are not the only service with success potential. Bus, train, boat and airline tickets follow the same patterns. Additionally, business professionals and other frequent travellers have a growing need for mobile services. Time has become one of the most valuable resources of today's business people. Therefore, all services that enable more time to be spent with family and friends are welcome. Push technology enables business professionals to receive reminders on their mobile terminal which suggest ticket purchases. This way, the people who travel regularly between two points are able to configure the ticketing service to remind them when they need to order their tickets.

▪▪ CASE STUDY

Galileo International Inc.

Galileo operates one of the largest computerized travel reservation systems in the world. With the emergence of mobile commerce, Galileo and its wholly-owned subsidiary, Trip.com, are concentrating on mobile solutions for travellers. The service enables travelers to re-book and monitor the status of flights using WAP-enabled mobile terminals, PDAs or two-way pagers. In addition, the service is able to notify the user when flights are delayed or cancelled.

Mobile reservation is another field full of promise. Imagine how easy it would be to get online with a mobile phone and reserve a table at your favorite restaurant. Location technology will lift services to a new level because consumers are able to search for restaurants and hotels nearby. Additionally, they will be able to subscribe to advertising services that send suggestions during lunch according to their location. Location-based reservation services will most likely be targeted initially on business professionals, often out of town. This way, they could search for the closest restaurants, hotels and car rentals without knowing anything about the city. This could be easily integrated into loyalty schemes and programs offering premium services to regular customers. They could access a free WAP service providing the closest location of hotels or car rental companies. With the progress of location-based technologies, they could also order a taxi from a hotel to pick them up without knowing their exact location.

Restaurant, hotel and car rental reservations require advanced networks and online presence from the companies offering such services. Therefore, most restaurants do not intend to go mobile within a couple of years. This might change with the arrival of advanced mobile terminals as restaurants are able to use them for accepting reservations. The initial investment for a restaurant is, therefore, likely to be very low. Additionally, mobile operators are able to hasten terminal adoption by offering out-of-the-box solutions for these types of companies. Whether restaurants see mobile reservations as one of their core customer service components remains to be seen.

Hotels and car rental companies are the ones with immediate potential. They are already using the internet actively and it is becoming one of their core components for conducting business. Customer relationship management has experienced a tremendous change with the arrival of the internet. In many cases, over 50 per cent of all the reservations come through the internet. Therefore, mobile channels will most likely become one of the important ways of serving travelling customers.

CASE STUDY

Hotelguide.com

The WAP version of Hotelguide.com enables consumers to look for hotel information using a mobile handset. The service is targeted for travelers in an unfamiliar city needing an accommodation immediately because of unexpected changes in travel timetables. Hotelguide.com has over 60,000 hotels around the world listed in their database with detailed information, but the WAP version is scaled down for better usability.

Travellers are able to access Hotelguide.com by entering the direct settings into a WAP phone or subscribing to some of the services provided by portal affiliates such as France Telecom and Swisscom. The procedure of finding a hotel is simple: First, the user types in a city and/or a hotel preference. He may also choose information to be displayed in one of several languages. Second, the traveller chooses a link from the list to acquire additional information about the hotel, such as price, telephone numbers and address. Third, he is able to place a direct call to a hotel and book a room.

➤ Later, the service will enable direct bookings. Customers with a personal profile on Hotelguide.com are able to use the WAP service without inserting their credit card number during the session because hotels will receive the payment information automatically from Hotelguide.com. This way, confidential information is not transmitted during the session and usability of the service is enhanced. Some future development issues are ability to search for hotels according to location of the user.

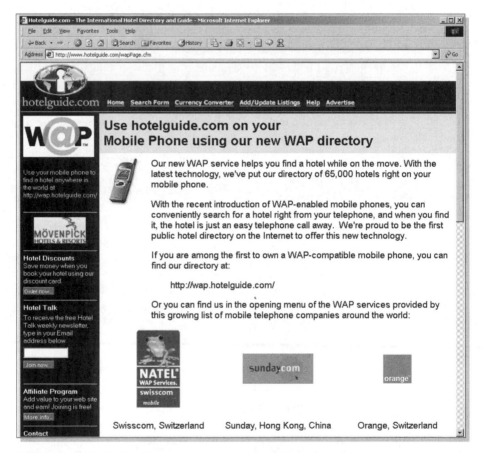

FIGURE 3.6 ■ Hotelguide.com can be accessed using a mobile phone

Entertainment

Custom ringing tones and icons

Ringing tones and icons are some of the early success stories of mobile entertainment. Users load these small files onto their mobile phones in order to customize the device and distinguish their ringing tone from all the others. In counties where mobile phone penetration has already reached 70–80 per cent

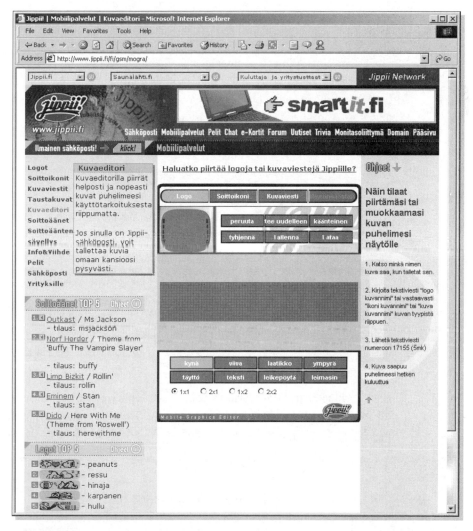

FIGURE 3.7 ■ Jippii, a Finnish internet Service Provider has a program on its web pages that can be used to draw an individual piece of art that can be sent to a mobile phone

of the population, custom ringing tones are actually very useful. Additionally, there are very strong motives of belonging and being a part of the group behind the use of custom ringing tones. Most young people want to download hit songs onto their mobile phone in order to demonstrate their style and opinions. Some older people may choose to compose a song or draw an icon of their own for creativity and humor.

:: CASE STUDY

Akumiitti, Finland

For a long time, Finnish companies have been pioneers in mobile applications. This is partly because of Nokia and its strong influence in the country and partly because of high mobile phone penetration. According to Statistics Finland, nearly all Finns from age 15 to 39 use a mobile phone. Forty per cent of men and 20 per cent of women over 60 years of age have adopted a mobile phone. Additionally, 78 per cent of Finnish households owned more than one mobile phone by the end of 1999. Around 90 per cent of the users send short text messages daily.[1]

A Finnish software developer Akumiitti is marketing its Entertainment Service Center (ESC) directly to mobile operators. Using the product, operators are able to offer downloadable ringing tones, logos and icons for subscribers. Games and the possibility to chat with other users of the service are introduced later on.

Entertainment Service Center enables users to listen to and compose ringing tones for their mobile phones using the fixed internet interface. Ringing Tone Composer can be customized to meet the graphical requirements of each individual operator. Short messages are used to download the ringing tones from the internet to a mobile handset.

Using an Icon Editor, subscribers can design and save their own custom icons that are also downloaded onto a mobile phone via SMS messaging. The same icons may be used both in Picture Messaging and as Caller Group Icons or Operator Logos.

The process of downloading custom ringing tones and icons is very straight-forward. Consumers with a fixed internet connection are able to compose or draw a unique piece of art and send that to their mobile phone. Another alternative is to choose a ringing tone or icon from hundreds of possibilities that can be browsed using a fixed internet connection. Because the majority of users are young people, the most successful items are, naturally, hit songs.

Games

Young people are the most active group of mobile phone users in terms of short messages, custom ringing tones and icons. Therefore, mobile games have great potential to become the next killer revenue generator for mobile operators. Until now, mobile games have been a part of the operating system. The emergence of new terminals equipped with micro-browsers has opened up new possibilities to offer mobile multiplayer games via the internet. User adoption has been slow because the current circuit-switched networks are expensive when used for games as the connection has to be open all the time. Therefore, the player has to pay for the data call even when waiting for the other person to make a move. Packet-switched networks and new terminals will revolutionize the mobile games industry because the player pays only for the transferred data. This way she is able to participate in multiplayer games for several hours without having to pay for time, only for transferred data.

Game manufacturers are also developing solutions for networked games. Nintendo, Sony and Sega have plans to link their existing game terminals to mobile networks. On the other hand, third party developers are already making several downloadable games for Java 2 Micro Edition, Symbian OS, Palm and Pocket PC.

▪▪ CASE STUDY

NTT DoCoMo in Japan and Sony Computer Entertainment Inc.

The Japanese mobile operator, NTT DoCoMo and Sony, the maker of PlayStation, are developing mobile entertainment services for Japanese markets. NTT DoCoMo has become famous for its successful i-mode service which has over 20 million subscribers using special handsets to access mobile internet services. The mobile network is based on packet-switched data and, therefore, the services are convenient and inexpensive to use.

NTT DoCoMo and Sony Computer Entertainment are planning to offer online games, music and movies for DoCoMo's i-mode handsets, enabling high speed internet access. Sony is planning to start selling games software titles available for both PlayStation and i-mode handsets.

CASE STUDY

NTT DoCoMo in Japan and Bandai

Japanese gaming company Bandai and NTT DoCoMo are also developing mobile gaming products for i-mode handsets. In addition, NTT DoCoMo is cooperating with Sun Microsystems in order to develop Java-enabled mobile terminals. The games can be either downloaded into the handsets or played online against opponents anywhere in Japan.

Music

The music industry has already had a taste of mobile business with the huge success of custom ringing tones. The ringing tones have been the most successful application of mobile portal sites and the same consumer behavior is likely to continue. Among other features, the advanced terminals of the future will be able to download music from the internet. Multichannel strategies are likely to be used when providing services to consumers. This way, the radio station listeners could get online with their mobile terminals immediately after hearing a song to download it. The radio stations, being distributors of music, are, therefore, going to receive another channel for conducting business. On the other hand, Music Television, Viva and other TV music channels can use the same business model.

In order to enable mobile music, device manufacturers and consumer electronic companies are getting closer to each other. Samsung has already developed a MP3-phone and others will follow the same concept. Consumer segmentation is becoming an important part of mobile device manufacturing because consumers are looking for different features when making a purchase decision. Therefore, most big manufacturers will have phones capable of downloading and playing music within a couple of years.

Business models in music provision are likely to change fundamentally with the emergence of mobile music. Retailers will build online services that send a reminder when your favorite group has a new album out. In addition, there might be services selling electronic concert tickets together with downloadable music. Therefore, radio stations, TV and e-commerce companies are all looking for new business opportunities enabled by the development of mobile networks and terminals.

Samsung Electronics

Samsung Electronics has launched a mobile phone with a built-in MP3 player in Korea. The device has a 32MB memory capable of storing about 30 minutes of music. Music files are downloaded into the device's flash memory chip using a PC connection.

MP3 is a de facto audio format that offers near-CD quality of music files that have been compressed substantially for making distribution over the network faster and more convenient.

FIGURE 3.8 ■ Samsung has introduced a phone with a built-in MP3 player

Betting

Betting is likely to be one of the successful applications of mobile commerce because it is time sensitive and messages between the customer and the betting shop are short and precise. Additionally, it is suited for large horizontal target groups and provides extra excitement to football games, formula one races and other sports events. Similar to stock broking, betting enables outsiders to participate in the event and gives them another reason to follow development of the situation closely.

Mobile betting will be increasingly time sensitive. Participants are able to offer bets in the middle of games and races, enabling them to respond to changes and situations immediately. In formula one races, for example, when someone has to drop out after five laps, the better is able to use his mobile phone to reconfigure the bet according to predefined rules.

While mobile betting has high expectations, there are some challenges as well. Scalability of networks and other infrastructure face growing demands because thousands of mobile terminal users might want to place their bet at the same time within a limited geographical area. If there are ten thousand people at a stadium who want to re-place their bet after a goal, what will happen to the mobile network capacity? There are likely to be another ten thousand people watching the game on television that would also like to reconsider their bets. Assuming that the mobile network at the stadium is able to handle ten thousand concurrent users, what happens to the system at the betting shop when twenty thousand concurrent users rush into the system and reconfigure their bets? Will it crash and burn? Maybe. Will it slow down? Most likely. Therefore, scalability of time sensitive solutions for a large audience require special attention.

CASE STUDY

Eurobet

The online sports betting service, Eurobet, offers a WAP-based betting service to their customers. Using their existing user ID and password, they are able to access wap.eurobet.co.uk to place new bets. The simplified user interface has been taken into consideration while customers are offered a wide range of sports betting opportunities.

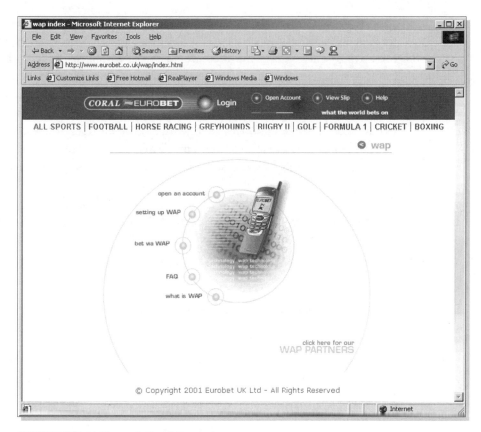

FIGURE 3.9 ■ The website of Eurobet

Financial services

Stock broking

Internet-based stock broking is one of the applications that has transformed traditional value chains. Stock broking has experienced a tremendous change with the emergence of electronic commerce because consumers do not need the services of traditional stock brokerages any more. They are able to invest online and read relevant news headlines directly via the internet. Additionally, the fierce competition of stock broking and lower transaction costs of the internet have decreased service fees substantially. Therefore, the number of online investors increases daily as consumers are becoming more and more interested in buying stocks.

Mobile evolution and the increased interest in stock broking are going to bring new, innovative service concepts to the market. Stock brokerages are looking for ways to differentiate and increase customer loyalty while the margins from basic services are dropping. Therefore, mobile solutions in markets with high cellular penetration are a natural migration path towards value added content and services. Since mobile terminal penetration is higher than fixed internet penetration in some countries such as Italy, mobile stock broking agencies are able to reach new customer segments. This way, the volume of online stock broking is also likely to increase with the emergence of the new channel.

Some main characteristics of mobile stock broking are:

➤ time-sensitive alerts and notifications based on predefined factors such as price-movements;

➤ real-time, personalized news headlines;

➤ instant advisory services;

➤ portfolio management and quote checks;

➤ buying and selling.

CASE STUDY

EQ Online in Finland

10,000 customers of EQ Online are able to access their WAP service in order to buy and sell stocks with their mobile phones. They can also receive numerical and graphical data along with stock exchange announcements. In addition, customers are able to activate an alarm service, informing them when a stock breaks a stipulated price barrier.

The security of the service has been taken care of by SmartTrust technology based on Public Key Infrastructure (PKI) using digital signatures.

FIGURE 3.10 ■ The website of EQ Online

Banking

Electronic banking has been the most important part of lowering customer service costs for most of the banks operating in areas with high internet penetration. It is also an improvement to the customer who doesn't have to leave home to take care of daily banking routines. The growing penetration of mobile handsets enables banks to offer the same services to a broader customer base today and in the future. Therefore, mobile banking services will be one of the most successful applications of the mobile era. Furthermore, m-banking is one of the basic applications enabled by mobile commerce because most severe security challenges will be addressed with its development.

There are two main reasons for the strong anticipated growth of mobile banking: fast penetration rate of handsets and the emerging use of banking services via the fixed internet. Since consumers have been quick to adopt fixed internet banking, it seems logical that m-banking is also going to embrace the same growth percentages. In several surveys, mobile banking has also been one of the most desired applications by the consumers.

The key characteristics of mobile banking can be divided into two different categories: basic services and advanced mobile services. The basic services include the same functions found in fixed internet banking applications.

Typically these are:

> account and credit card balance;
> recent transactions;
> interest and exchange rates;
> funds transfer;
> bill payment.

However, these basic services must be optimized for a small screen and limited text input capabilities using pre-filled forms and streamlined processes.

Advanced mobile services are ways to differentiate and create additional customer loyalty. They are designed specifically for mobile users offering location-independent and time sensitive instant messages and integration to mobile shopping services.

Some of the advanced mobile banking solutions are:

> automatic balance notification according to predefined limits;
> credit line notifications;
> downloadable exchange rate calculator;
> instant consumption credit agreement;
> direct integration between mobile merchants and banking services.

∷ CASE STUDY

Nordea, Finland and Sweden

Nordea (formerly known as MeritaNordbanken) has been a pioneer in electronic banking services. It started out with telephone banking in 1982 and continued to PC banking in 1984. Text message-based mobile banking was introduced in 1992 and Web banking in 1996. WAP bank of Merita opened its doors in 1999.

The success of web-based banking in Finland has been enormous. In a country with a population of five million people, Merita has well over a million active users of internet banking services. This is partly because of high fixed internet penetration and partly because of early market entry and effective customer education. Internet banking is generating substantial cost savings every year with lower transaction expenses and reduced resources in physical customer service units.

The high mobile phone penetration of Finland and Sweden has encouraged Nordea to emphasize WAP services. Customers are now able to access and perform the following functions:

> check balance;
> view recent transactions;
> make bill payments;
> perform fund transfers between two accounts;
> check bill due dates;
> check Visa card transactions;
> stock and share trading;
> customer e-mail;
> view news.

The success behind Nordeas electronic services has always been early market entry and management commitment together with high internet and mobile phone penetration in Finland and Sweden.

Standardization issues

There are numerous standards bodies and organizations that are developing solutions for mobile security, banking and payments.

Mobey Forum, an industry consortium established specifically for mobile banking and brokerage, has been launched by Nokia, Ericsson and Motorola. Some other members are Barclays, Citigroup, Deutche Bank and Visa International. Mobey Forum aims to develop open standards in areas such as payment, remote banking and brokerage.

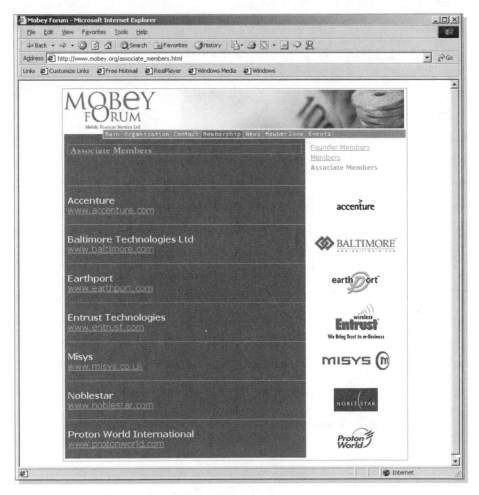

FIGURE 3.11 ■ The website of Mobey Forum

Mobile Electronic Transactions initiative (MeT) was set up in 2000. It aims to promote open standards in m-commerce and security. Even though the two initiatives overlap in some areas, Mobey Forum is focusing on mobile banking and MeT aims to develop mobile commerce in general.

Radicchio alliance was established in September 1999 to promote Public Key Infrastructure (PKI) as a standard for secure mobile commerce transactions. It was initially launched by EDS, Gemplus and Sonera.

CASE STUDY

Halifax Plc, The United Kingdom

Halifax has given its customers 150,000 WAP phones, free of charge, when signing up for a credit card and a checking account. They are able to access their personal bank account details with a WAP phone.

Mobile payments

Mobile payments are used to pay, not only for merchandise purchased via a mobile channel, but also for transactions in the physical world. The key driver for mobile payments is the widespread adoption of mobile handsets and a trend towards digital cash. The most active players in the industry are mobile operators, financial institutions and device manufacturers who all have their own interests to drive the future into a direction they desire. Mobile operators would like to become the middlemen between the consumer and merchants, collecting a small cut for providing security and debt recovery. Financial institutions see mobile payments as one of their core competencies since they have traditionally provided consumers with solutions that enable them to pay for products using credit and payment cards. Device manufacturers' primary concern is a threat of slow development of payment methods that respectively slows down demand for mobile phones.

Mobile operators are well positioned in the value chain as providers of micropayments because they have a regular billing relationship with consumers. Therefore, they are able to act as clearing houses by providing payment solutions for merchants at their mobile portal. The billing is very convenient for the customers as they receive a regular bill from a company they trust and using the services does not require the additional effort of filling in cumbersome forms with a mobile handset. All the information is already there because the customer is recognized and identified by the operator. Mobile operators are also offering payment services for a variety of companies that, traditionally, have had nothing to do with mobile technology.

Among others, these are:

- vending machines;
- car wash machines;
- jukeboxes;
- toy car rides;
- copy machines;
- passport photo machines.

The machine is equipped with a transmitter that is connected to a mobile network. The consumer calls a certain number in order to activate the machine and the specified amount of money is automatically added to his personal debit account with the mobile operator. This way, the consumer is able to buy soft drinks, use public copy machines, and take photos for his passport without having to carry coins. There is another perspective for this. Collecting coins is a relatively expensive part of operating many small ticket machines. For example, hundreds of parking meters have to be emptied regularly because the container for the coins is filled within a short period of time. The coins are heavy and full-time workers are required to empty the meters. Additionally, numerous coin slots of parking meters are broken every month as a result of vandalism and theft. As the price of mobile transmitter units decreases, mobile operators are offering services to enable convenient ways to pay for parking using a mobile handset. As a result, operating costs are decreased and thieves will lose their incentive to break into parking meters because a coin slot does not exist.

Financial institutions have been showing innovative solutions as well. Some banks have established mobile portals in cooperation with several merchants where consumers are able to pay for purchased items using an existing online bank account. Consumers are able to access the services regardless of their mobile operator because they dial directly to the servers of the bank. However, they have to be customers of this particular bank in order to make mobile purchases.

Financial institutions, especially credit card companies, are likely to benefit from the maturation of Bluetooth technology. A mobile device that is equipped with a smart card provided by a credit card company is able to use a Bluetooth link for transferring a payment. The cash register checks the credit limit and other information automatically while debiting the money from the user's account. Also, smart cards with downloadable digital cash can be used for instant payment when Bluetooth technology becomes available.

CASE STUDY

Sonera Mobile Pay

Sonera Mobile Pay enables consumers to purchase various goods and services such as refreshments, passport photos and a car wash using their mobile phone.

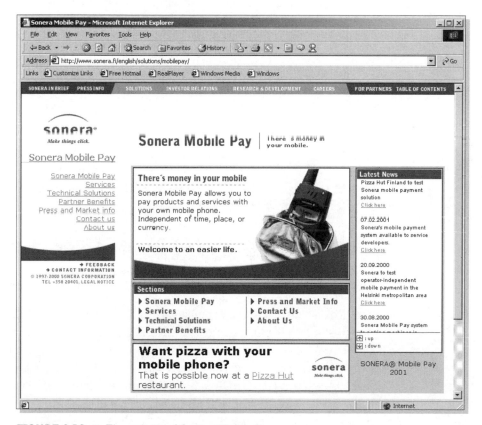

FIGURE 3.12 ■ The website of Sonera Mobile Pay

There are three ways to purchase products:

➤ Dial a premium rate number.

➤ Dial a premium rate number with a prefix. This enables corporate phones to be used privately for paying for items. There are two separate bills, one for corporate phone calls and one for private purchases.

➤ Pre-standing agreement with Sonera to charge the items on a credit card. After the call has been made, the vending machine or car wash is activated.

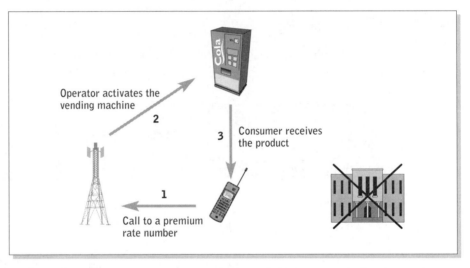

FIGURE 3.13 ■ The mobile payment method provided by an operator does not need a financial institution to provide authentication

CASE STUDY

Electronic Mobile Payment Services (EMPS)

Nordea, Nokia and Visa are developing EMPS to enable secure mobile payments using dual-slot mobile phones with chip cards. The first slot is for a normal SIM card which takes care of routine telephone services such as caller identification and telephone number retrieval. The extra slot is meant for banking transactions and includes a tiny credit card. Combined with Bluetooth, EMPS can be used to facilitate a wide array of mobile transactions ranging from vending machines to purchases in a local supermarket.

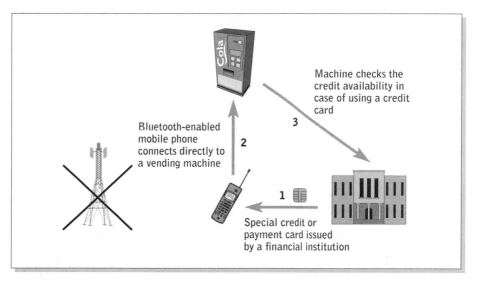

FIGURE 3.14 ■ Bluetooth takes control away from mobile operators because financial institutions are able to issue their own payment cards. However, the distribution of new payment cards is somewhat problematic because financial institutions cannot control the distribution chain of mobile handsets

Other innovative solutions

Many companies are already offering mobile terminals to all employees. This way, communication is enhanced as everybody can be reached regardless of their location. The widespread adoption of mobile handsets enables innovative services generating operational cost savings. For example, monthly pay slips can be sent electronically to all employees. Companies with thousands of workers are able to save substantial amounts of money, distributing the salary information electronically instead of sending it though the postal service.

Instant messages can be used to provide information about the direct debit services provided by banks. The customer receives a notification when a new bill has entered into the system. Additionally, information about due date, sum and origin of the bill is displayed in the message. This way, the customer knows the status of electricity, telephone and other bills without having to enter into the actual payment process.

Advertising

The limited user interface of mobile devices has caused many to doubt the viability of advertising. This is a logical conclusion if mobile advertising would be similar to the banner ads of the fixed internet. The opinion has roots in the false expectation that mobile internet services would be similar to the applications used with a fixed internet connection. However, mobile internet will be totally different from fixed internet services. There will be a strong emphasis on personalization, time sensitivity and location-based services. Therefore, mobile advertising will find new, dynamic and innovative ways of conveying messages to a consumer.

There will be around one billion mobile subscribers by 2003. As most of them will have a personal mobile phone within hearing distance where ever they go, there are enormous possibilities for targeted, one-to-one advertising. The growing importance of location-based services and personalization will cause rapid development of mobile advertising that offers products and services to match the needs of individual consumers. Kelsey Group, a market research firm tracking advertising trends, has predicted that wireless advertising revenues could reach $17 billion by 2005 when there will be 192 million mobile phones in North America[2].

Until now, fixed internet banner advertisers have used several ways to target their message to a correct user segment. Some of them are:

> user profile of the service, such as financial and sports news;

> search engine keywords;

> time targeting for time sensitive items, such as lunch;

> domain targeting (geographical and company-level targeting);

> database targeting in services requiring registration and login.

The era of mobile advertising will differ from fixed internet campaigns because the emphasis on search engines is smaller and local content becomes increasingly important. Additionally, multichannel advertising strategies will become more significant because the limited user interface of mobile terminals cannot be used for filling long forms. Therefore, fixed internet, TV, radio and print becomes integrated with mobile advertising combining the strengths of the various media into one package. One of the most important technologies regarding mobile advertising is automated settings configuration which enables the internet settings of a mobile phone to be reconfigured within seconds. For example, by sending an instant message to a certain number, the consumer is able to order new internet settings for her mobile phone immediately. The settings are sent via instant messaging and the user can reject or install them directly. After that, she is able to access new content and services without reconfiguring the phone. This way, advertisers are able to use a multi-channel approach for delivering personalized, location-based and time sensitive content to mobile phones. Some examples are:

➤ instant ordering for items advertised on TV and radio;

➤ location-dependent advertising based on user profiles created using the fixed internet;

➤ sponsored information delivery channels;

➤ time-sensitive alerts such as sponsored traffic reports, concert and movie ads.

CASE STUDY

mSpot service in Hong Kong

Peoples, a PCS operator in Hong Kong, has launched a service called mSpot that uses location-based advertising in return for subsidizing free calls to its subscribers. This is a win-win situation for both parties since advertisers have an opportunity to precisely target the ads according to the location and profile of the user and consumers are able to make free calls in return for listening to the advertisements.

The cost of purchasing a prepaid subscriber identity module card is approximately $6.40. After installing the card, calls are free according to the number of ads the user is willing to listen to. One 10-second ad enables one minute of local outgoing airtime, up to a maximum of six. When the user is making a phone call, the service asks how many ads he is willing to hear. After listening to the ads, the call is placed.

Each base station is able to broadcast a separate ad. Because the country is densely populated, base stations in Hong Kong are close to each other. Therefore, the approximate range of one base station is 0.6 miles and the ads can be targeted rather precisely. This enables solutions where movie theaters send advertising messages to people in the immediate vicinity.

➤

➤ The selling and targeting of the ads is taken care of by Spotcast, a company specializing in location-based advertising. The revenue for the service is shared between Spotcast and Peoples.

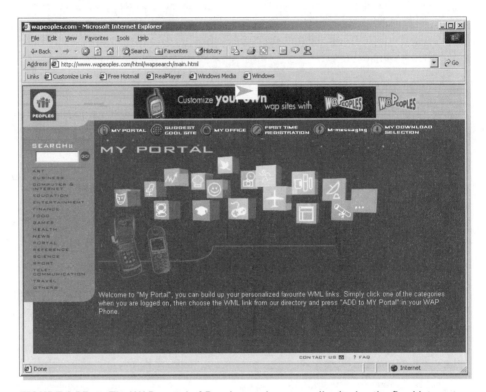

FIGURE 3.15 ■ The WAP portal of Peoples can be personalized using the fixed internet

▦ CASE STUDY

SpeechWorks International

SpeechWorks develops systems for allowing advertisers to reach consumers over the phone. The user is able to skip spoken advertising messages which are seldom longer than six seconds.

Geoworks Corp.

Geoworks, one of the leading providers of mobile commerce and information services for the consumer market, has launched a mobile portal called Mobile Attitude that allows consumers to select which kind of advertising messages they are willing to receive. Users are able to receive news, weather and sports using their mobile device. Additionally, the portal offers personal reminders and advertising promotions.

Telematics

Telematics is a broad term for the wireless data and voice systems used in vehicles, normally in combination with the Global Position System. Because 70 per cent of mobile calls in the US are made in vehicles, telematics has a very strong success potential in the era of 2.5 and 3 generation mobile services. According to a study by The Strategis Group, there will be 11 million telematics subscribers in the US by 2004. The same report predicts that revenue from telematics will increase from $40 million in 1999 to more than $1.7 billion in 2004[3].

Some of the applications offered by telematics are:

- roadside assistance;
- emergency services, such as automatic airbag notification;
- remote engine diagnostics;
- location-based navigation and maps;
- mobile commerce applications such as traffic reports and ticket reservations;
- stolen car tracking;
- remote door lock and unlock;
- concierge services.

Automatic speech recognition is one of the applications capable of revolutionizing telematics because, that way, the fundamental problem of safety could be overcome when using data services while driving. However, the applications are still very sensitive to foreign accents and noise so the widespread adoption of speech recognition has not taken off yet. Additionally, mass market speech recognition applications require heavy processing power from the servers so, the deployment becomes more expensive and difficult than deployment of normal data services.

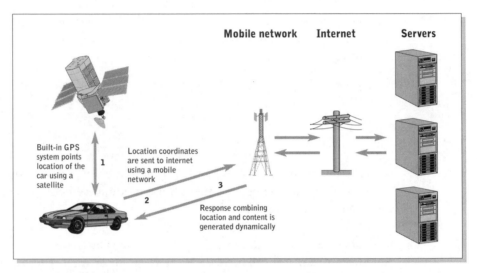

FIGURE 3.16 ■ Location-based telematic solutions use GPS technology to locate a vehicle. Location coordinates are sent to the internet and a response is generated by combining location coordinates into content, such as maps and driving directions

CASE STUDY

Ford Motor Co.

Ford is aiming to equip more than 1 million new cars and trucks with telematics systems by the end of 2002. Additionally, by the end of 2004, virtually all new cars and trucks will be equipped with telematics. Ford has established a venture called Wingcast in partnership with Qualcomm to develop technology and services for cars of the future. It also has a deal with Sprint PCS to provide data and voice services to some Lincoln 2001 models. The applications include voice-activated calling, emergency and roadside assistance and internet services.

News and information

Mobile information providers are faced with a difficult question: Why should a subscriber access paid content with a small screen mobile phone instead of using free channels with superior user interface capabilities? Is the information so important that it has to be accessed immediately instead of waiting for alternative channels? These are some of the fundamental questions which will determine the potential success of mobile information services. Since most of the initial mobile portals are based on information provisioning, the questions will soon be answered.

There are two types of services currently available: push and pull applications. Using pull services, the subscriber accesses portal content by sending a short message, with a keyword, to a certain number. Another alternative is to use a WAP phone for browsing information at the mobile portal. In contrast, push applications are sent to a subscriber automatically according to pre-configured settings. The user is able to subscribe to instant push services providing daily jokes, news, TV program listings and numerous other services by sending a short message to a certain number. This way, the messages are sent on a regular basis daily, weekly or when something special happens. For example, financial push services can be used to send messages to subscribers when news concerning their personal stock portfolio companies hits the markets. Naturally, personalized services are usually configured using a fixed internet interface.

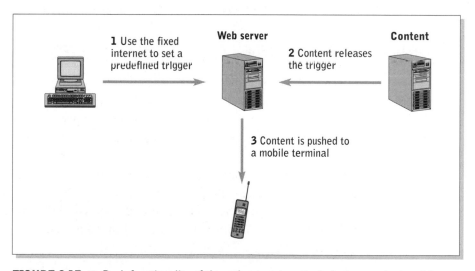

FIGURE 3.17 ■ Push functionality of the web server is activated when content matches the predefined specifications

Multichannel approach for mobile commerce

It is very unlikely that customers will use their mobile devices for surfing the net in the way we understand it today. Limited screen size, clumsy input methods and cost are the main reasons why this will not happen. On the other hand, a portable device with user authentication and security functions is an ideal way to finalize transactions. Therefore, retailers should focus on multi-channel strategies which combine the best features.

Most mobile phone users carry them wherever they go. They have it on a table when watching television. It is beside the steering wheel when they listen to the local radio station in the car. The phone is conveniently carried around in a belt bag when they walk on the streets, read newspapers or browse the internet. How can marketers avoid the temptation of developing innovative concepts for a device like this? That's right. They can't.

However, a mobile phone is a very, very personal device. Therefore users do not tolerate any additional, disturbing messages without prior request. As most people do not actively search for advertisements, marketers have to find polite ways to communicate their offerings to consumers. This can be done through television, radio or the internet. Later on, marketers could try using existing channels to enter into the mobile commerce area but it has to provide additional value to the receiver. This value could be free calls, free location-based services or even discount coupons for the local supermarket.

How to use television for mobile commerce?

People in countries with high mobile phone penetration are already used to multichannel strategies that overcome the limitations of mobile devices. TV commercials present competitions and games where viewers can participate using their mobile phones. By sending a short message to a particular number, you can participate in a competition held in a local supermarket. The message is expensive, typically around a dollar, but, amazingly, there are always some people who want to take a chance to win that awesome prize. The revenue from the service is divided between the mobile operator and an advertiser. To be analytical, why are conservative, reserved Finns for example, participating in such competitions?

➤ It is extremely convenient to take your phone and dial the number you see on the screen.

➤ The competition is an adventure in the middle of passive listening and watching. There is a great feeling of entertainment involved in the action.

➤ The whole process takes less than a minute, so the person acts on impulse.

It is possible to send a short message to a particular number and, in return, receive communication settings for a mobile portal or any other internet page. This function will enable multichannel advertising, where TV is used as a motivator and internet pages, tailored for mobile devices, are used for further information and transactions. The process goes like this:

➤ TV commercial for a dirt cheap Caribbean holiday is presented.

➤ "For additional information, send a blank short message to an 800 number"

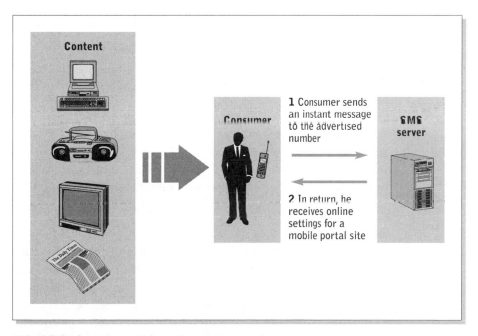

FIGURE 3.18 ■ The workflow of multichannel advertising

➤ After three seconds, you receive the settings for your mobile phone.

➤ You activate the settings and contact the internet site for further information.

➤ At the site, you are able to book the holiday immediately. The payment can be sent with the confirmation or you are able to pay directly using online banking.

With multichannel advertisement, time is money. The whole process is over in a couple of minutes and both of the parties are (hopefully) happy. For the consumer, this is a major improvement in comparison to advertising in which you have to remember internet domain names. With domain names, the real problem is not to remember the name, but to move from your comfortable couch in order to get connected to the fixed internet. Usually, this does not happen and response rates for TV commercials remain low. Partly because of that, most e-commerce sites focus on internet banner advertising, enabling a direct response with a single click. Even then, only a small percentage of viewers bother to click through the banner. TV advertising, combined with a mobile channel, is able to reach millions of people at the same time while still providing an instant response channel.

Use radio to reach mobile people

The combination of radio and mobile commerce could be a powerful marketing tool. Small ticket goods and services, especially, have great potential to become successful. The ubiquity of the mobile phone can be used to target travellers since most people listen to radio in a car, train or bus. Therefore, items suitable for mobile customers can use radio as another marketing channel.

However, radio listeners are different from TV viewers in the sense that they usually concentrate their attention on other things besides listening. Therefore, radio advertising for mobile commerce should be clearly articulated with a direct invitation. It should focus on time and location, right here, right now, with a message strong enough to wake up the listener. For example, car drivers could be targeted in a rush hour with a direct offering: "Would you like to receive traffic alerts directly to your mobile phone? Call number 500 to activate the service." After the telephone call, location-based traffic alerts could be offered to the driver. The alerts could be pushed to the mobile phone, offering alternative routes or intersections. This way, the driver would be able to avoid the traffic jams before entering them. In addition, an alternative route could be shown on the screen of the mobile phone.

What are people usually listening to on the radio? What is the main component in every show, with every single radio station? Music. Therefore, the mobile commerce targeted at radio listeners will certainly focus on the delivery of music. Samsung has already developed a phone with MP3 music capabilities. With the arrival of packet-switched mobile networks and new billing mechanisms, among other things, mobile phones will be used for music. Radio stations have an exceptional opportunity to offer music for mobile devices. "Would you like to buy some of the songs played at Hard Rock 99? Just call 12345 right now to receive settings for our music library. The song list will always include the 10 hottest hits and 20 songs played recently."

These were just a couple of examples showing the enormous capabilities of a multichannel approach for radio advertising. The limited internet browsing opportunities can be overcome by selecting an appropriate strategy for reaching customers. Some other examples for combined advertising are:

➤ location-based weather reports/alerts;

➤ video delivery with high speed third generation networks;

➤ location-based points of interest for car drivers and travellers;

➤ turn-by-turn directions for car drivers;

➤ hotel information;

➤ emergency and car break down services.

Listeners are likely to respond to offers either immediately or never. Without a direct invitation, they will forget the offer and the actions required in order to achieve additional information. For maximum results, they should be offered goods or services that answer an immediate need.

▪▪ CASE STUDY

ewireless

While Americans spend around 500 million hours in their cars every week, radio advertising produced 17 billion dollars in revenues in 1999 according to the Radio Advertising Bureau. Until now, radio advertising has not been interactive like banner ads on the internet. However, the situation is subject to change due to the growing penetration of mobile phones in the market. While consumers are driving to and from work, advertisers have an excellent opportunity to offer shopping services to this large, captive audience.

➤

➤ ewireless, a Chicago-based start-up company, creates interactive advertising services for driving consumers. Commuters are able to dial #333 to talk to a live operator patching them over to an advertiser when they hear a radio commercial or see a billboard. In return, advertisers are able to send coupons, additional information or even initiate an over-the-phone sale immediately. The call is free for the consumer, who does not have to pay for airtime or have minutes deducted from calling plans. Because the whole process is done using a voice call, as far as a handset is concerned, there are no special technical requirements for the service. Therefore, everybody with a mobile phone is a potential user.

The service has strong potential for movie and concert tickets, books, CDs and other inexpensive items that can be purchased in an impulse manner.

Where is the synergy of the internet and mobile commerce?

The birth of the internet and electronic commerce is without a doubt one of the most important advances in the economy since the invention of the steam engine. Traditional electronic commerce has introduced lower transaction costs, improved supply chain integration and independence of a geographical location. Companies around the world have been able to communicate at lower costs and contact each other regardless of time. Additionally, electronic intermediaries have been able to rationalize the value chain resulting in improvements in efficiency and lower prices for end users.

Believers in electronic commerce have been excited to see the emergence of mobile commerce. According to general assumption, mobile commerce will follow the business models of electronic commerce by providing increased independence of location and time. This would lead to mobile shopping any-where, anytime. However, the characteristics of a mobile phone do not support "surfing" as we understand it today. Mobility, ubiquity, instant con-nectivity and intimacy of a mobile phone, together with obvious limitations regarding screen size and input methods, cause changes in the business model. Mobile phones will not be used for internet browsing. They will be used for immediate information retrieval, impulse buy and communication.

However, the network infrastructure in terms of back-end systems, servers and security procedures is likely to remain similar to electronic commerce. Therefore, companies with deep skills in electronic commerce have a head start in developing new services and concepts for future terminals. The emphasis has to be focused on personalization and location technologies, enabling time sensi-tive delivery based on the needs and position of the consumer.

Internet merchants can use mobile devices in order to build stronger customer relationships through providing value added services. Online stores are able to benefit from the new technology because they can be in contact with their customers regardless of their location.

These online services with time sensitive information will be most likely to benefit from the multichannel approach, combining mobile and electronic commerce. In addition, mobile channels with time dependent personalized alerts are a way to increase customer loyalty and differentiate one online service from another. Therefore, push technology will play an important role in future services. With push technology, you are able to create solutions that cause customers to be excited to get back to the Internet pages of your company. What are these services?

Scenario 1

I have just bid 1,000 dollars for a digital camera at an online auction. While doing so, I checked the box saying "Please send updates to my mobile handset". Now, I receive a message to my mobile phone telling me that someone has raised the bid to 1,100 dollars. Additionally, the message has default answering options: would you like to:

➤ retire;

➤ raise the bid by 50 dollars;

➤ raise the bid by 100 dollars;

➤ raise the bid by 200 dollars.

Because there are only five minutes until the end of the auction, I decide to raise the bid by 100 dollars. After five minutes I receive another message confirming that I made the highest bid. In addition, the message contains payment details with the deadline. I enter my online bank with a mobile phone to transfer the money right away.

Scenario 2

I am a busy businessman. To keep up with the development of semiconductors, I have personalized my web portal to provide information about that particular field of industry. Also, my participation in the board of directors of a company called Asian Circuit Inc. compels me to know the industry news as soon as it hits the market. In recent months, there has been a surge in the number of mergers, leaving us in a position where the larger companies are able to dominate the market. Because of the critical situation, I enter the web portal and order the breaking news directly to my mobile phone. This way, I can leave for a holiday with peace of mind and be informed as the situation changes.

Scenario 3

I ordered books from another country via the internet. Because I have an exam on Monday, I ordered the books to be sent directly to my home. The online store has a service agreement with the delivery company using new technologies. Therefore, I receive a notice to my mobile phone two hours before the books arrive. This way I know when to be home to receive the books.

Scenario 4

I have an account with a local bank which uses mobile and electronic commerce to improve their customer service. I have personalized my bank account settings online. When the balance of my bank account drops under 500 dollars, I receive a notice to my mobile phone.

Scenario 5

Because I am an extremely enthusiastic fan of a band called Groovy Brothers, I am willing to buy their next album as soon as it becomes available. However, they have not revealed the date when it will be released. Therefore I enter my favorite online store, personalize the website and register to receive a message when the new Groovy Brothers album will be available. After a couple of weeks, I receive a message to my mobile phone telling me that the album is available today. To make the purchase, I visit the website again.

These are just some of the ways to use multichannel strategies in order to increase customer loyalty by providing value added mobile services. To benefit from the multichannel approach, merchants have to pay attention to the strengths of both channels. A mobile channel is able to provide time sensitive and intimate content regardless of the location of the handset owner. The fixed internet can be used for filling long forms, viewing images, reading product specifications and many other tasks hard or impossible for a mobile device.

How do you attract the audience of print media?

Since Guttenberg, print media has been an organ for a mixture of views around the world. Whether they are political, financial or social, opinions have been communicated through this traditional media. Additionally, newspapers and magazines provide us with news, education and entertainment from the various fields of life. Reading a newspaper has very strong emotional and cultural ties, so it has been able to retain its position in the middle of the electronic content explosion. However, many newspapers and magazines are already using the internet as another channel for their customers. This way, they are able reuse content and provide customers with additional information about issues that have been reported. Additionally, an internet interface has been able to cure the limitations of time sensitivity and interactivity of traditional printed matter.

In order to understand mobile opportunities in this area, let's take a look at the characteristics of newspapers and magazines.

Newspaper

➤ bulky;
➤ time sensitivity at a day level;
➤ local information and news;
➤ local ads;
➤ short stories;
➤ no interactivity.

The daily newspapers are bulky and require some space for a convenient reading experience. Therefore, they are usually read on a kitchen table with a cup of coffee. Since the paper comes every day, it is an ideal marketing tool for companies with direct, time sensitive ads. Additionally, ads are typically characterized by region because most subscribers prefer to know what is happening in their community. This is the reason why companies advertise daily commodities in newspapers. The interaction level of a newspaper is very low, because by its nature, it does not offer an instant way to respond to messages. Therefore, some newspapers have established internet portal services to provide more interactivity and generate information about their customers. Those newspapers are also offering access to real-time news and related topics online. From a marketing point of view, banner ads are sold in order to cover the costs. By clicking them, the customer is able to access the marketers' website directly.

Magazine

➤ small and portable;

➤ time sensitivity in a week/month level;

➤ less local than the newspaper;

➤ national/international ads;

➤ detailed stories;

➤ no interactivity.

Magazines are smaller and more portable than newspapers, so they can be read on a train, bus or in a car. Time sensitivity is usually less important in magazines since they are published on a weekly or monthly basis. Magazines are also less dependent on location. National and international companies post their ads in them to increase brand awareness. Interactivity is similar to newspapers. It does not really exist. Different from newspapers, characters and goods and services are usually the cover stories.

Mobile devices are able to compensate for some of the limitations of the print media. On the other hand, mobile channels could also be used to complement the special characteristics, such as time sensitivity and regionality, of magazines and newspapers. Here are some of the examples.

Scenario 1

Jeff is reading his favorite sports magazine on the way to his parent's house. For a long time, he has planned to invest some of his extra money in stocks. Unfortunately, he doesn't quite know how to start and to whom he should turn. Additionally, he has the impression that all stock brokerages are really expensive. Surprisingly, there is an ad in the magazine which tells everything about prices, service options and starting procedures. The company also has an online service for mobile terminals that can be activated by sending a blank message to a certain number. After sending the message, online settings are sent to the mobile terminal. Jeff activates the settings, goes online and finishes his application. His phone is using a Wireless Identification Module for security and authentication. Therefore, both he and the stock brokerage know that the trading is safe. After reading the beginner's guide, he is ready to start investing.

Scenario 2

Amy is reading the daily newspaper on the kitchen table. Avington's Mall is having the annual Crazy Sales Day. Some of the Crazy Day products are pre-sold via a mobile channel where you can select the product and keep it reserved until 2 a.m. Amy is so excited about a set of special earrings that she gets online and reserves the product. To do that, she doesn't have to leave the table because the mobile terminal is right beside her. After breakfast, Amy gets dressed and heads to the mall. She is happy to see the earrings before making a final decision. They look just perfect.

Scenario 3

The local Pizza Taxi is launching a new service. Customers can order online using a mobile channel. The cooks have their mobile terminals ready for new orders all the time. This way, they are able to respond to customer requests directly, without delay. Additionally, the online service can be maintained with a low cost because the restaurant only invests in the mobile terminals and an online interface maintained by a mobile phone. The local newspaper is the most obvious place to advertise because, this way, the restaurant can reach their target audience. As there are no online transactions involved, security is not a critical issue.

Scenario 4

Amy is having a terrific time with her favorite car magazine. She enjoys a story about the latest model of Ferrari. On the last page, there is a competition where the main prize is to win a Ferrari for one day. The only thing Amy has to do is to get online with her mobile phone and vote for the best stories of the month. This way, the editors are able to know what kind of stories the readers are interested in. So, Amy takes her mobile phone, gets online and votes for the story about Ferrari.

The common denominators for all these stories are instant online access, convenient use of a mobile terminal and the combination of print and a mobile channel. Some of the scenarios could be possible without the print media, but multichannel strategy is more effective because the limitations of mobile terminals can be overcome. Print media is able to cover the limitations of the small screen by providing a wealth of information in a convenient way. Therefore, the combination of print and mobile create easy to use, interactive services accessible anytime, anywhere.

Mobile services will be characterized by impulse action

Right here, right now

Mobile commerce will combine new technologies and bring internet connectivity to our fingertips regardless of our location. However, that internet is different from fixed internet surfing with colorful pictures, wide screens and fast keyboards. Rather than a scaled-down version of the fixed internet, the mobile internet is something totally new and different. Having limited screens and text pads, mobile terminals will be used for services with short, time sensitive and personalized content.

Mobile commerce will be characterized by convenience with an emphasis on customer experience. The customer has the power to decide which services he wants to use. The settings are changed in a matter of seconds if the customer is not happy with the portal or a service he is currently using. Therefore, service providers should focus on value added services, creating increased customer loyalty. Additionally, the services should strengthen the sense of community and belonging.

The ubiquity of mobile phones, together with a zero boot time, causes impulsive use of the devices. Whether it is a mobile phone or a PDA, it is always close to the user, always on and always connected. Therefore, mobile commerce will be characterized by impulse buys and services answering the user's current needs. Location-based services have a great potential, because they are able to provide information for impulsive use. Additionally, the messages are short and thus fit onto the small screens of the mobile devices. There are, generally, two types of services, push and pull, depending on the user's action. In a pull service, the user requests the information and gets the result according to his location. "Where is the closest ATM?" is a typical pull service. Push services are more complicated, because the location of the user has to be known at all times. Additionally, personalization is needed in order to customize push messages. Location-activated advertising with a message "Walk 100 meters ahead and turn right to participate to our amazing summer sale!" is an example of a push message. By nature, mobiles services are local and personal. Therefore, the location-based technology is one of the essential components of successful service.

The right here, right now approach can also be achieved by deploying multichannel concepts which combine a mobile channel with radio, television, print or the internet. Multichannel marketing models with a direct invitation have great potential because of the ubiquity and instant access of a mobile device. Therefore, a customer reading his daily newspaper is able to contact the advertised online site without leaving his chair. An advertiser is presenting the offer in the newspaper, and the customer only goes online for a transaction. This way, both media are used for optimal results. A mobile channel offers interactivity and security. Newspapers are able to present the information more completely.

Fast transactions, short messages, alerts

The workflow for a shopping process has to be short and precise, so the usability of the customer interface needs to be considered very carefully. Devices may have screens with four rows of text and a normal, 12-pad "keyboard" for character input. Using a form factor like this, the buying process needs to be based on short messages and fast, easy to fill forms. In the case of complicated transactions, a multichannel approach should be deployed. Then the user would have pre-filled forms, prepared online with a web interface and the mobile device is only used for finalizing a transaction.

Personalization is one of the ways to improve the customer interface. With personalized service, default form values are already there, making it possible to close deals and commit transactions faster. Security of a personalized service becomes critical in cases where credit card numbers and other highly sensitive data are given as default values. Another driver for personalized solutions is better usability when browsing for product categories and searching for information. The consumer does not have to browse as much as without personalization because information and products are displayed according to his preferences.

Personalized, time sensitive alerts will be crucial in the mobile environment. Financial services, online stores and mobile portals can use alert services for customer loyalty, differentiation or revenue generation. Alerts are always push messages, sent when a certain trigger is released. This trigger may be a date, time or value set by the user. The alerts are always time sensitive, so they fit perfectly into a mobile environment.

These are some examples of alert services:

- **Real estate:** "The apartment with the characteristics you specified has been found!"
- **Recruitment:** "There are four new jobs in the service matching your specifications."
- **Team working:** "You have a meeting with Nicole Johnson in the ballroom in 5 minutes."
- **Communication:** "You have new, high priority mail."
- **Location-based:** "Drive slowly. There is an accident 5 kilometers ahead."
- **Logistics:** "The items you ordered are now at the Livington sorting office. You will receive the products at approximately 9:00 a.m."
- **Warehousing:** "The number of items in the inventory has increased to 12,000."
- **Retail:** "The book you pre-ordered is now available. For ordering instructions, follow the link"
- **Stock Market:** "This is a real-time financial news service: 1 new message, priority high, published 5 minutes ago. Message: Nokia and Ericsson have decided to merge. Suggestion: Carefully watch the stock price of Motorola. For further details, follow the link."
- **Welfare Services:** "Joe Hamilton has requested help from village drive 2. Call 4343434 to talk with him."

Notes and references

1. Paul Quigley, "In Finland, It's All About Wireless," Wireless Week, www.wirelessweek.com (June 26, 2000).

2. Deborah Méndez-Wilson, "Wireless Mall Lures Advertisers," Wireless Week, www.wirelessweek.com (May 8, 2000).

3. Brad Smith, "Wireless In The Driver's Seat," Wireless Week, www.wirelessweek.com (February 21, 2000).

4

Corporate applications

Aligning mobile commerce with your business goals

Streamlined business processes can be developed by integrating mobile applications with existing systems. Aligning mobile channel with business goals and strategies is important in order to benefit from the new technology. Existing technologies and procedures can be used to provide information to the mobile environment if legacy systems are up to date and flexible. In the future, several applications in the corporate intranet and extranet will have mobile extensions, enabling employees and partners to access time critical information regardless of their location. Mobile commerce will also transform organizations causing impulsive communication and faster processes as people can be reached regardless of their location.

How does the mobile internet transform your organization?

As noted earlier, some key characteristics of mobile commerce are ubiquity, intimacy and time sensitivity. Corporate applications are likely to follow these features by introducing time sensitive, personal solutions that enable real-time access to corporate databases. Therefore, corporate communication will be totally renewed with the emergence of mobile applications and developed terminals. Employees are able to access their e-mail as soon as it reaches the inbox. Actually, e-mails are pushed directly to mobile terminals resulting in faster decisions and improved efficiency. Business professionals are no longer tied to their offices as they can be notified as soon as new information arrives. Because of the increased impulsiveness of a mobile channel, we will see some fundamental changes in the business culture. The coming change could be compared to the emergence of e-mail in recent years. How many modern organizations can afford to be without e-mail nowadays? The same transformation will happen with the emergence of mobile instant messaging.

Instant communication and access to corporate databases from mobile devices will make demand forecasting easier. Several fields of business are heavily dependent on accurate forecasting, especially when the products are time sensitive or connections to subcontractors become a critical success factor. Products with a very limited window of opportunity have to be transported to the customer as soon as possible. Therefore, correct timing will become increasingly important. Correct timing is critical in manufacturing as well. In order to reduce inventories and cut down fixed costs, companies optimize the time for raw material delivery. Raw materials have to be ordered just in time to maximize production capability and minimize costs. This way, connections to both subcontractors and resellers are increasingly time sensitive. In many cases, a mobile channel will be one of the tools that helps companies forecast demand and rationalize communication among the parties.

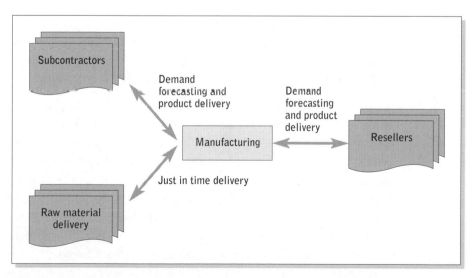

FIGURE 4.1 ■ Transactions become time critical as the number of intermediaries in the value chain increase

Mobile phone manufacturers are heavily dependent on their subcontractors. The demand for certain components has to be well known beforehand, otherwise manufacturing cannot be optimized. Having a relatively short window of opportunity, a certain model has to be transported to the reseller as soon as it is commercially available. Additionally, the device manufacturer must be able to forecast the demand appropriately, otherwise the subcontractors are not able to deliver the components in a timely manner. Communication with the reseller is critical in terms of demand forecasting. In the future, even the smallest telephone shops can be connected to the central system by using mobile technology. It may be a mobile terminal or a networked cash register that the reseller is using to update the databases on the central system. This way, the demand for the products can be monitored in real-time and forecasting becomes more accurate.

Another time sensitive field of business operation is internal and external customer service. With the emergence of the internet, customers have become more impatient and they expect to be responded to within hours of submitting a request via e-mail. Companies frequently lose customers because of slow and unprofessional customer service. Therefore, customer relationship management has become one success factor and a key value driver of a modern company. What will happen to customer service when most consumers are equipped with internet-capable mobile terminals? Will customer service gradually fade away because the new technology is able to solve our problems? This will not be the case. The importance of customer service will be underlined and delays will not be tolerated. In the era of mobile commerce, consumers submit their complaints and questions to the company using the terminal. They then continue with their everyday routines and expect to be answered promptly.

The mobile internet will transform the concept of working and leisure time. In the era of the internet, the number of mobile workers has increased tremendously because new team working tools can be used with a laptop computer regardless of location. Additionally, most companies that provide laptops to employees expect e-mails to be checked at least a couple of times a day. The emergence of the new, internet-capable terminals will fundamentally change organizational behavior. The terminals are likely to be substantially cheaper than laptops, so they can be distributed to all personnel. As e-mails are pushed to terminals in real-time, employees are expected to take immediate action when the message arrives. This makes business more efficient. At the same time, however, policies and procedures are needed in order to protect personnel from trivial junk mail. The boundary between working and leisure time has been in transition since the internet enabled remote working. The same phenomenon will accelerate with the emergence of the mobile internet. People are using the same devices for communication regardless of their location. They receive messages related to work when they are at home and vice versa. The concept of working hours becomes increasingly broad.

In general, the mobile internet will intensify the evolution that has begun to take place in the era of the fixed internet. The same patterns will remain, with an emphasis on time sensitivity and location independence.

Things to consider before deployment

Taking a strategic approach to mobile commerce

No organization should consider implementing mobile applications just because they are becoming more popular. The decision should be based on clearly identified needs and business requirements to create additional value and draw the company closer to the goals and objectives defined in their main strategy. Performance gaps and opportunities to create additional value should be examined first. The appropriate solution can then be introduced. A mobile channel is one of the possible solutions but there are many others as well Therefore, the characteristics of a mobile device should be taken into consideration during the planning process. The small screen, slow text input and low processing power of a mobile terminal are factors that limit possible applications. On the other hand, the invincible aspects of a mobile device, like ubiquity, timeliness and intimacy enable unique solutions for a corporate target group.

What is your core business? What are the most important factors that enable you to succeed and develop your business? Where are the biggest gaps in terms of technology, processes and human performance? These are some of the questions that have to be asked and answered in order to benefit from mobile commerce. They help in aligning mobile channels with your core competencies and reaching the full potential of mobile commerce. Additionally, the identification of value drivers is essential to explore the full potential of the new technology. Value drivers are factors which make the performance of a business better.

Some possible value drivers in an organization can be:

- improved human performance;
- fast inventory turnover;
- reduced inventories;
- cost savings;
- increased productivity;
- higher product quality;
- efficient collaboration with subcontractors.

Mobile commerce, aligned with value drivers and business strategy, is able to improve the overall performance of a company. Therefore, strategic decisions and the deployment of mobile applications should be in line.

One of the biggest impacts of electronic commerce has been reduced transaction costs and virtual integration of value chains. Business partners and several intermediaries of the value chain are now able to connect to each other's databases and review information relevant to them. With internet technology, companies are also able to develop closer business relationships, resulting in improved performance and better partner collaboration. In addition, electronic commerce has had a significant impact on internal processes. Employee self service, virtual human resource management and employee training are just some of the fields where electronic channels have proved to be efficient. The emergence of mobile applications is able to bring new features to existing services. Companies with high mobile phone penetration are able to introduce new corporate applications that have been integrated with the existing back-end systems. This way, employee self service, messaging and human resource management applications can be used regardless of time and location. Strategic partnerships between the different parties of the value chain can also be strengthened with mobile commerce. This way, electronic commerce and virtual integration of the value chain gets another channel. Business partners are able to access time critical information in back-end systems using both the fixed internet and mobile devices.

TABLE 4.1 ▦ Integration of value chains

	Action	Implication
Value drivers	▪ Define the value drivers of the company ▪ Assess the impact of the new technologies to the value drivers	▪ The company is able to align mobile commerce applications with the most critical value drivers
Strategy	▪ Define corporate strategy ▪ Understand the strategic context of mobile applications	▪ Better understanding of the business requirements of mobile commerce applications ▪ Increased management commitment ▪ Envisioned migration path for the applications
Competitors	▪ Closely follow the actions of competitors	▪ Consider their actions and make decisions based on your own applications
Core business	▪ Define the core business of your company ▪ Acknowledge the core processes	▪ Mobile applications can be developed to serve the most important processes of the company
Internal processes	▪ Based on the core business, define the most important internal processes ▪ Observe the processes to define gaps or opportunities ▪ Define internal value drivers	▪ Use mobile applications to solve the gaps and realize opportunities ▪ Focus on internal value drivers to determine whether a mobile channel could be used to create additional value
External relations	▪ Define the gaps in relation to the virtual value chain integration ▪ Address the needs for enhanced communication ▪ Define external value drivers	▪ You are able to define possible ways to use mobile applications in order to enhance communication and commit transactions

Define and analyze your goals

After defining the internal and external value drivers, the goals are determined. Naturally, objective setting takes place to ensure that all the processes are serving the overall strategy of the company and the value of core business can be maximized. A mobile channel should be aligned with the strategic context to understand the business requirements and ensure management commitment. This way, the migration path to the next level can also be defined beforehand.

A mobile channel can be used to serve various business goals. Many of them have sub-goals that realize the main objectives. In many cases, industry characteristics and business requirements define the objectives. Therefore, there are several different approaches when using a mobile channel to improve the performance and generate cost savings.

The structure of an objective setting could be something like this:

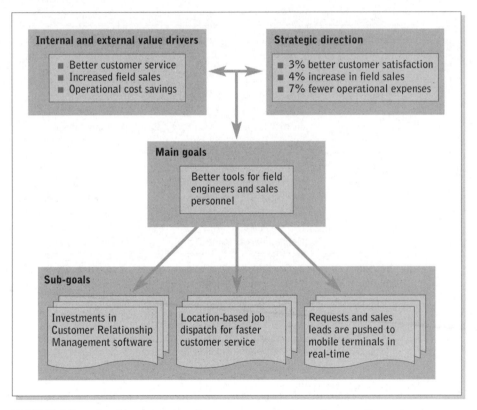

FIGURE 4.2 ■ An objective setting for a company wanting to increase the customer service level

Vertical and horizontal target groups for mobile applications should also be defined. Vertical targets are typically narrow user segments, such as field service engineers or sales representatives. Horizontal applications are meant for a massive number of users. Mobile e-mail, for example, could be an application for a horizontal target group. Initially, most of the mobile applications are targeted at vertical users. This way, the efficiency of a mobile channel can be tested with lower costs and feedback is used to develop applications further. Objective setting for these two groups is fundamentally different. In most cases, horizontal applications serve general business goals and highly defined strategies. Some horizontal goals could be improved communication and streamlined processes in horizontal procedures, such as travel management and time entry. Vertical objective setting is more detailed. Business unit strategies and the needs of individual departments are usually the main drivers behind vertical applications. This way, highly customized applications are offered to a narrow user segment. The goal can be better customer service or increased efficiency among certain professionals. Horizontal and vertical objective setting is also different in terms of management commitment. As horizontal applications serve a large number of users and are specifically aligned with the strategic goals of the company, they usually attract more interest. Therefore, horizontal solutions have strong management commitment. In contrast, vertical objectives cannot attract the same attention which makes the applications less visible. However, vertical target groups are vital to the overall business and can be used to examine the efficiency of mobile applications in general before the implementation of expensive horizontal solutions.

Setting a timetable is the logical step after defining vertical and horizontal goals. It really depends on the development of mobile networks and terminals, so, the company should follow developments closely and define the appropriate entry requirements before development takes place. Additionally, a migration path for the existing applications should be defined according to the new features of the mobile terminals and networks. Being first is always more expensive than following the crowd. Timing is a vital part of a company's strategy. If a mobile channel is seen as one of the key value drivers in the future, investment is justified. Otherwise, the company should start slowly from the vertical solutions and proceed towards horizontal applications as more experience and appropriate tools become available.

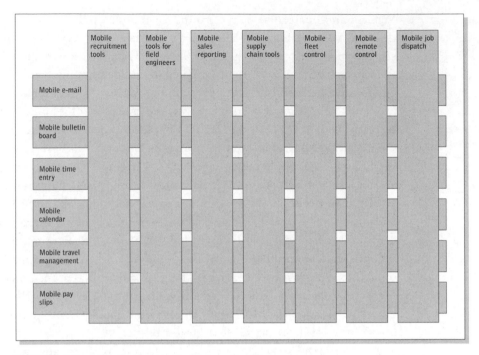

FIGURE 4.3 ■ Vertical and horizontal applications

Another important factor to consider before application development is the determination of success standards. Appropriate measures should be developed to estimate whether the application was a success or a failure. As well as measuring the result, the whole process has to be taken into consideration because the information is relevant to future development.

Integrating technology

Companies have very different conditions and prerequisites for entrance into mobile commerce. Generally, those equipped with modern back-end systems and electronic commerce solutions have better chances to succeed technically than the companies who have not yet explored the possibilities of e-commerce. Mobile commerce is based on e-commerce software architecture and network infrastructure. Naturally, some additional parts, such as WAP or an instant messaging gateway have to be installed in addition to the electronic commerce infrastructure. However, these changes are not the major task in developing mobile commerce solutions.

There are two ways to implement mobile applications for corporate use. Many software companies have developed mobile extensions for existing systems and these can be purchased and installed to provide information to mobile devices. For example, Lotus Notes and Microsoft Exchange have mobile extensions. Another way to deploy mobile applications is to hire software developers and systems integrators to build a custom application. In many cases, this is the only possible option because corporate systems are increasingly complicated and integration has to be carried out to make the application suitable for the special business requirements of a company. The largest effort of making a custom application is the software development which transfers information requests and responses between the back-end system and the mobile terminal. This way, the information in corporate databases can be reviewed and updated using a mobile handset. In many cases, the piece of software is developed using Java because of its platform independence and modular structure. That way, some of the Java components can be used later on with similar projects.

The mobile evolution path in corporate applications follow similar patterns to electronic commerce. Initially, the company does not have a mobile presence. The management does not have any experience with mobile applications and, therefore, readiness for change might be slow and characterized by third party opinions. The next level is reached when the company decides to purchase a mobile application, typically an out-of-the-box solution that integrates one of its existing systems into a mobile channel. For example, some employees may experiment with mobile e-mail that has been built by installing a software extension on top of the current mail server. An external WAP gateway, provided by a mobile operator, is used to reduce the time to market and decrease the amount of initial investment. After the piloting phase, mobile e-mail is extended to cover all personnel. At this point, management has an idea of the business case for mobile applications. They are also able to identify some of the opportunities, strengths, weaknesses and threats of mobile applications. With the development of technology, the company may choose to move to the next level by introducing several applications based on existing systems. Some possible services could be internal bulletin boards and office directories. This way, employees and management can acquire experience in mobile applications and develop scenarios for future solutions. The next level is reached when the applications are combined in order to create a corporate portal. Software integration becomes more important because the employees are now offered several applications for mobile devices. On top of the applications mentioned earlier, they can manage their personal information in the corporate databases, submit time

reports and manage travel reservations. At this point, the company may purchase an internal WAP gateway to enhance security. The final level in mobile
commerce is reached when integration becomes even more important. At this
point, location-based technologies are actively used by some of the vertical user
groups. Location-dependent fleet management, remote control and job dispatch are used to increase efficiency. Another important technology is instant
messaging. It is used in various time sensitive applications.

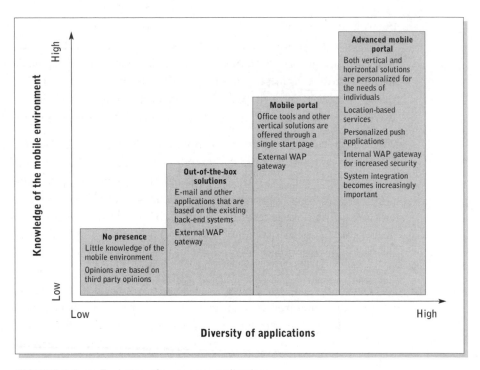

FIGURE 4.4 ▦ Evolution of corporate applications

Measuring success

Corporate applications cannot be measured in the same way that consumer
applications are evaluated. There are basically two different approaches
towards corporate measurement: value analysis and technical analysis. Value
analysis is based on defined business expectations and requirements that have
to be met in order for the application to be successful. Management sets the

indicators before application development takes place. At the initial stage of mobile application design, the value drivers of the company are based on strategy and core business processes. At that point, the value indicators for a mobile application should also be defined.

Companies use technical analysis to monitor the usage of the applications. Similar to mobile commerce, technical analysis is not very complicated. The challenge is to put the information into a format where trends and differences in an application usage can be identified. The log files of web servers are generally used to analyze the usage of e-commerce applications. The same files are generated when mobile applications are used because the information goes though a web server. Therefore, information about access times, concurrent users and transferred data can be processed and printed out for review.

TABLE 4.2 ▥ Some examples of value and technical analysis in vertical and horizontal target groups

	Value analysis	Technical analysis
Mobile e-mail	▥ User satisfaction ▥ Changes in organizational behavior (faster decisions, speed) ▥ Increase in productivity	▥ Speed of the service ▥ Number of active users ▥ Capacity to serve concurrent users ▥ Cost of upgrade
Mobile time entry	▥ Cost savings ▥ Streamlined operational process	▥ Correct integration with back-end systems ▥ Usability of the application interface
Fleet management	▥ Customer satisfaction level ▥ Speed of the delivery service ▥ Number of jobs per day	▥ Request response times ▥ Response times of the database
Mobile sales management	▥ Increased sales forecasting ▥ Streamlined processes ▥ User satisfaction	▥ Accuracy of the data ▥ Number of possible concurrent users ▥ Number of active users ▥ Security
Remote control	▥ Cost savings in reduced operational expenses ▥ Better sales forecasting	▥ Machine-to-machine response times ▥ Upgrading possibilities ▥ Service life
Mobile recruitment solutions	▥ Decreased response times ▥ Faster handling of applicants ▥ Location independence and increased mobility	▥ Usability of the service ▥ Functionality of predefined triggers ▥ Database response times ▥ Number of possible concurrent users

Horizontal solutions

A mobile channel is suited for dynamic and time sensitive applications. Because of the small screens and the limited processing power of the terminals, information should be precise and personal. As noted earlier, the era of mobile commerce will be characterized by a communication revolution. This is caused by real-time e-mail and other person-to-person communication tools. In addition to that, mobile commerce will embrace the concept of machine-to-person connectivity because many of the applications include watchdog features. Setting watchdogs, users are able to monitor the status of various issues while concentrating on something else. For example, executives may set watchdogs to notify them when some of the key figures in demand, supply or inventory are not normal. Using watchdog features in corporate systems, employees can receive a message when their travel plans have been approved by a manager. Recruitment professionals may set watchdogs to receive a notification when an applicant matching their criteria is entered into the corporate recruitment system. These types of applications and features are best suited for a mobile environment. Mobile commerce is one of the tools making business more dynamic, efficient and time sensitive.

There are still numerous industries where only a few office workers have PCs. Construction and factory workers, for example, do not necessarily need a computer in order to make working more efficient. If they have one, it is not likely to be a personal computer with e-mail and office tools. Remote workers may not be able to access the digital bulletin board or e-mail of the company. Mobile terminals, being substantially cheaper than PCs, will enable all employees to access the communication and information channels of the company. This way, management is able to reach everyone, regardless of their location or working environment. Additionally, employees that have traditionally been not able to use digital channels can now communicate with each other and their business partners.

The communication evolution towards mobile solutions enables interactive applications for knowledge management and centralized administration as well. Management is able to access the satisfaction of workers by sending a short form to all the employees. When the employees complete the form and submit it to the central system, the results are available within minutes. This way, management and employees have an opportunity to improve the working environment and interact regularly. Employee satisfaction forms are excellent documents to be distributed via mobile channels because the receiver does not have to type any information while filling the form. Check boxes, drop-down menus and radio buttons are used to hasten the process and increase the number of respondents.

Enterprise Resource Planning

Enterprise Resource Planning (ERP) is an industry term for a wide array of activities used to manage manufacturing or similar actions. With ERP software, a company is able to manage inventories, product planning, interaction with suppliers, order tracking, parts purchasing and some parts of customer service. Modern Enterprise Resource Planning packages have also introduced

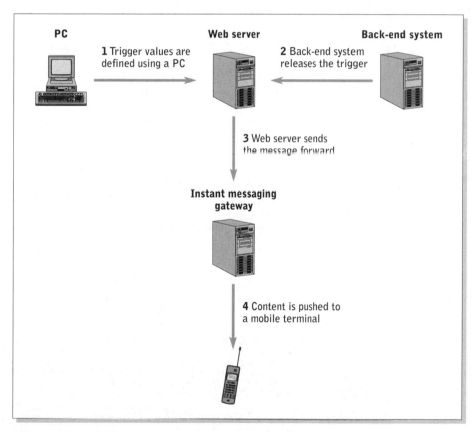

FIGURE 4.5 ■ Time sensitive watchdogs can be added to an ERP solution

modules for human resource management and finance. The software is typi-cally purchased in modules (e.g. inventory, order, human resources) and integrated with a relational database. SAP, Peoplesoft, Baan, Oracle and J.D.Edwards are some suppliers of ERP solutions. Recently some suppliers, including SAP, have introduced ERP outsourcing which enables third parties to take care of software management.

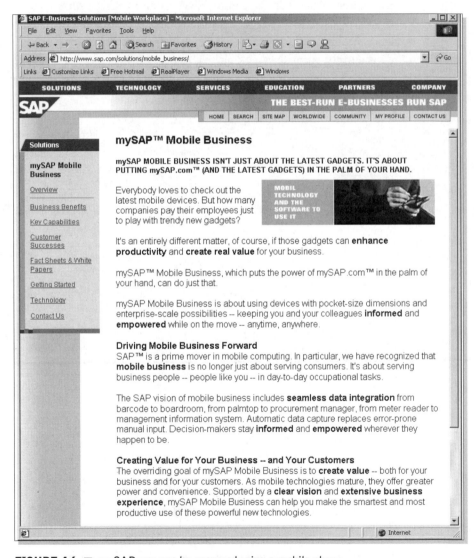

FIGURE 4.6 ■ mySAP.com can be accessed using a mobile phone

Enterprise Resource Planning software can be accessed using a mobile terminal. A company's customers may have limited access to the system and they are able to order goods using a mobile channel. However, the workflow of such an action has to be simplified since mobile terminals are not very convenient for inserting a lot of text. Therefore, the use of drop-down menus and radio buttons is recommended. Customer interaction could also be enhanced by providing an array of value added services. An ERP solution could send a notification to the customer as soon as the product ordered leaves the factory. This way, the customers know the status of their order and they are able to plan their own deliveries in a more precise way.

A mobile ERP solution can also be used to provide information internally. Sales representatives can monitor the stock situation constantly and inform the customer if they will receive the product immediately or if they will have to wait for delivery. Mobile workers can use ERP software to place orders and see the history and current situation of the client.

Another feature of an integrated ERP solution is a management reporting tool which provides time critical information about the key figures of the company. With a mobile management reporting tool, executives are able to monitor the processes of a company in real-time. Various watchdogs can be set and they are activated when certain figures increase or decrease to a certain level. The activated watchdog sends an instant message to the mobile terminal of the executive. This way, he is aware of the key figures regardless of his current location.

Customer Relationship Management

Customer Relationship Management (CRM) consists of methodologies, software and internet capabilities which help a corporation to manage customer relations in an organized way. A CRM application has a database that describes customer relations. It includes information about contacts, history, ratings and personal interests. This way, management, salespeople and service personnel are able to make more informed decisions about suitable products and sales offerings. A CRM solution can also be opened upto a customer. This way, he is able to order new products and review support information for the existing ones.

Mobility has been an important part of customer relationship management for a long time. Therefore, most CRM software providers, such as Siebel and Clarify, offer various deployment options for their products. Siebel, for example, has five deployment options ranging from PC to WAP-enabled mobile phones. This way, the field and office workers have an ideal set of tools regardless of their location or environment. Mobile data has become more important in recent years because the development of mobile networks enables new, innovative concepts. More and more business is now being conducted outside of traditional corporate walls. With mobile terminals, companies are transferring their business information to the locations where transactions actually occur. Marketing departments are able to identify and target the best customers and generate quality leads with information provided by the mobile salespeople. In addition, sales management is able to forecast the demand because information from the field is always accurate. Operational and administration costs are cut as duplicated processes can be streamlined because information inserted at the client site doesn't have to be typed into the system again.

FIGURE 4.7 ■ Siebel, the leader in customer relationship management software, has launched Siebel Wireless allowing access to corporate data with WAP-enabled mobile phones

Salespeople are some of the most highly leveraged workers in a corporation. Incremental revenue in sales significantly increases the bottom-line revenue of the corporation. Manufacturing and numerous other processes are totally dependent on sales. Simplistically, profitability of a company is based on two main issues: extensive sales in the upper part of the value chain and cost savings focused on primary processes such as manufacturing and administration. Mobile devices should be used to realize both of these goals.

Maintaining customer satisfaction depends, partly, on shortened cycle time from order to delivery. Response and confirmation time is shortened when mobile terminals are used by customers and salespeople. A salesperson is able to close deals and make orders at the client site. The customer can receive order confirmations on his mobile device and respond to them immediately. As a result, order processing is streamlined and optimized for the various needs of the client organizations.

With a mobile CRM extension, a salesperson is also able to perform the following tasks:

- access inventory availability and convey the information directly to the customer;
- interact with customers, suppliers and management with a real-time connectivity;
- provide on-site price quotes;
- confirm appointments;
- access personal information management tools such as contacts and calendar;
- maintain personal sales records.

Field service is another important part of mobile customer relationship management. While traditional voice-based dispatch works in some smaller companies, large corporations with a massive number of field engineers and mechanics are able to generate substantial cost savings by implementing mobile data solutions. A centralized call center is used to receive customer requests and insert them into a corporate database. The requests are automatically dispatched to field workers based on their skill profiles, location or pre-defined customers. The field worker receives the new request as soon as it is inserted into the system. Before heading to the customer, he updates the status of the request to assigned. This way, the system does not assign a new job to him.

At the client site, he is able to browse information about customer history and other issues relevant to service delivery. Using a mobile terminal, he can also order spare parts and forecast the time needed to repair the machine. Before heading to the next job, the field engineer updates the status of the request and takes care of billing procedures. This way, the workflow of service delivery can be constantly monitored and information for billing is generated automatically. Management knows the locations of the field workers and they have a wealth of statistical information in the central system to plan for future improvements.

The advantages of mobile field services are:

- faster response times;
- less resources needed at the call center;
- improved dispatching process;
- streamlined workflow;
- increased efficiency of the field workers;
- more statistical information available for planning;
- accurate and fast billing;
- less paperwork – less duplicated processes;
- improved communication;
- on-site technical support and trouble shooting databases.

Supply Chain Management

Supply Chain Management (SCM) is an industry term for managing the flow of finances, information and materials among suppliers, manufacturers, wholesalers, retailers and consumers. It is actually overseeing the value chain and its different intermediaries. The ultimate goal is to reduce inventories by optimizing material and information flow without sacrificing service level – there have to be enough products in the inventory to satisfy demand. Industries with short invention and product cycles, such as high tech and consumer electronics, are highly dependent on supply chain management to interact with their numerous suppliers and retailers.

Mobile devices can be used to optimize the flow of information and materials. An increased number of mobile workers and time sensitivity drives companies towards advanced mobile solutions. There are two types of SCM solutions:

planning applications and execution applications. Mobile terminals are used with execution applications to provide information about the status of goods and payments. Because most processes are time critical, SCM software can be configured to inform the parties if something does not match expectations. For example, a purchasing agent can receive a message if materials needed for manufacturing are in danger of running out.

SCM applications with open data models are capable of sharing data both internally and externally. This way, the key suppliers, manufacturers and retailers share the same information which optimizes time-to-market of the products and reduces costs. Planning becomes easier as everybody in the supply chain knows the status of the others. Another trend is web-based procurement marketplaces where parties can trade materials and make auction bids with suppliers. Naturally, these solutions are highly time sensitive, so mobile terminals can be used to monitor and receive instant messages about the market situation and partners. Web-based procurement sites can offer services in which the user receives a message automatically when the price matches the offered materials. This way, demand and supply meet without human intervention and only the final step of payment has to be taken care of by the company.

Remote control

Mobile remote control can be used across industries to decrease operational costs, provide security and enhance customer service. The components of remote control utility are normally a GSM, TDMA or CDMA unit, battery, built-in antenna and, possibly, a GPS receiver. The GPS receiver is used if the equipment needs to be located. The Yankee Group predicted, in 1999, that the number of telemetry units in service would grow more than 500 per cent over the next five years. The growth is likely to be very fast in sectors such as health care, security, transportation, utilities, municipal services and atmospheric control.[1]

Remote control units can be used for various tasks:

- Automated data reading and reporting from water-power stations, oilfields, electrical networks and other distant or inaccessible locations.
- Automatic defect control and reporting for high volume machinery such as copy and vending machines.
- Traffic control systems.

➤ Publicity panels.

➤ Weather stations.

➤ Location-based vehicle tracking.

➤ Automatic defect control and reporting for cars and trucks.

Remote data terminals are best suited for locations where traditional phone systems cannot reach, as installing them exclusively for data transmittance purposes would be too costly. Remote surveillance is ideal for machines that are geographically scattered over a large area and require regular service. For example, vending machines can be taken care of according to sold items. There is a remote control unit inside the machine and a sensor that sends a message to a central system when one of the items sells out. This way, employees fill the machines only when it is necessary.

Remote control is also used for security purposes. Mobile monitoring can be implemented in boats, trucks, cars and buildings where wired telephone lines do not exist. At the time of alarm, a remote control unit sends an instant message to the police, a security company or the mobile phone of the owner. Cost effective and easy to implement, remote security systems are likely to see an increased demand.

▪▪ CASE STUDY

WebLink Wireless Inc.

Isochron Data Corp is an application service provider offering telemetry solutions for ice distribution and vending machines. The system, called VendCast, allows vending operators to remotely acquire critical information about their vending machines. Therefore, customers of Isochron are able to save on operating and personnel costs while the company maintains a high customer service level. The solution distributed by Isochron can be used to acquire information about inventory level and equipment health among other things.

Mobile self service

Mobile self service is an electronic way of handling various corporate administration duties. For companies with an extensive number of field workers, it is able to provide employees with an easy and convenient way of handling administrative duties. There are clear advantages to this. The administrative costs related to paperwork can be cut down and workers are able to take care of simple tasks without leaving the site. As a result, operational costs decrease and field workers become more efficient.

By using mobile travel management, an employee is able to access information about flight and train schedules, hotels and car rental services. After finding appropriate means for travelling, the services can be booked using a mobile terminal. The bookings can also be sent to management for acceptance. The manager immediately receives the inquiry through a mobile network and can accept or refuse the reservations by return. This way, communication between the manager and employee becomes faster and decisions can be made within minutes. Therefore, mobile terminals enable travel management to be taken care of rapidly, conveniently and with less bureaucracy.

Another solution adapted for mobile terminals is personal training management. An employee is able to submit her personal skill profile and future development challenges to the corporate system. The system can dynamically send push messages to a terminal of the employee if there is an appropriate course available. This way, the employee can concentrate on other duties while the system monitors all the information about training courses available. Watchdogs like this are suitable for mobile terminals because the owner is always close to the device and the limited form factor does not enable convenient "surfing".

Using a mobile terminal, employees are also able to update their personal information in the corporate database. Updating bank account information, address and emergency contacts is a small task for the worker, but organizations with thousands of employees are able to save substantial amounts of money by offering a mobile channel for that. Some other small applications for mobile self service are simple administration duties such reporting travel expenses and short ordering forms for lunch vouchers and similar issues.

Examples of vertical corporate markets

Construction

Construction workers may not be accustomed to using a computer at the construction site. Compared to PDAs, PCs require a certain level of background information because the use of applications and peripherals is more complicated. PDA devices are suited better for the construction environment because of their easy to use interfaces and small sizes. Zero boot time and instant data connectivity are other strong points for PDAs.

Construction workers seldom have an office where they keep records of their contacts, their addresses and phone numbers. Additionally, asset management is virtually non-existant, because there are no tools for that. Therefore, companies with multiple construction sites suffer from inefficiency and underutilization of assets because of communication failures. Construction sites have to have a wide selection of tools that are not necessarily needed all the time because sharing them is inconvenient and time consuming. In addition, duplicated processes and extensive paperwork increase administrative costs.

Mobile solutions in everybody's pocket can make the construction business more effective. Workers are able to access the corporate database to locate tools and utilities needed at the construction site. Using a mobile terminal, they plot the new location of all the assets they use and move. This way, all employees can access the location of the closest assets when they need them. As a result, redundant assets can be eliminated and use of the existing ones is optimized.

Construction workers are able to manage their personal contacts, calendar and messaging applications using a mobile terminal. Each evening, they log digital reports to the central system, describing activities and working hours. These reports are automatically processed and distributed to project management. Management is then able to identify and describe the progress of the project. Employees may have access to an online ordering system where they are able to place orders using a mobile device, so most routine administration is taken care of. The device is also a powerful communication tool because suppliers and management can always reach individual workers.

Emergency and healthcare

In many situations, communication is a crucial part of delivering effective healthcare or emergency services. The professionals have to be available for colleagues, patients, patient family members and several other parties, such as insurance companies, regardless of their location. In addition, their access to medical records and various other resources is becoming one of the competitive advantages for various companies.

Mobile data solutions are targeted for:

- doctors, ambulances, visiting nurses;
- physicians;
- psychiatrists and psychologists;
- police;
- fire stations.

Private hospitals can use portable terminals to increase the efficiency and service level of mobile workers. A hospital with several dispersed properties is able to maintain the resources and assets with a central information system. The system can be used with a handheld computer, accessible from an ambulance or anywhere else. Based on the information in the central system, ambulance workers know beforehand which hospitals have doctors available to offer appropriate treatment. They can avoid time-consuming mistakes that cost the lives of the patients.

Visiting nurses are able to receive their next assignments using a mobile terminal. Before entering the homes of their patients, they can also review medical records and get additional information about medicines and dosage instructions. The call center uses mobile data solutions to control multiple workers at the same time. Representatives are able to provide better customer service because they can monitor the status of workers in real-time and forecast the arrival times better. Another improved area is billing because all patient related costs are captured at the point of care. A company knows exactly how much time has been spent with a certain patient.

Instant messaging and cell broadcast can also be used for communicating critical emergency situations to individuals or masses of employees. Cell broadcast is used to send the same message to all employees within a certain area. This way, policemen and firefighters can receive notifications in real-time and access resource databases for additional information.

In some countries, fines are imposed based on salaries. Therefore, police officers have to phone a call center every time they impose a fine on somebody. This ties up a lot of resources and increases operational expenses. Using a mobile data solution, police officers could access the databases for information about salaries. This way, the process of fining can be streamlined and hastened.

Location-based services are able to provide security and efficiency to a mobile workforce. With a location-based solutions, the call center is able to assign new jobs depending on the location of vehicles. For police, this means faster response times and the ability to control ongoing situations in real-time. Because the call center knows the location of each police car at all times, even when there is a chase going on, it is able to manage critical situations better. Security is also enhanced in unexpected situations.

Finance

Investment banks and brokerage houses are becoming increasingly dependent on information systems. The emergence of e-commerce has shaken the industry, causing lower margins and competition from new entrants using the internet in a dynamic way. Information technology enables companies to respond to customer orders, price changes and market news immediately. Now the same information and services are available using mobile terminals as well.

For mortgage and stock brokers, a desktop is no longer the only way to access time critical information. Mobile terminals, such as PDAs and cell phones, enable direct access to personalized stock quotes and corporate information. In the financial industry, push applications are becoming increasingly important because busy professionals do not have time to constantly monitor the stock markets, so watchdogs or electronic triggers are used. The broker can set certain limits on stock prices or interest rates fluctuation. If the limits are reached, a message is sent to the mobile terminal of the broker enabling her to respond to the changes immediately. This way, the broker can monitor the interests of her clients in real-time without being at her desktop all the time. News feeds and industry reports can be sent to her mobile terminal in the same way. If a sales representative doesn't have to stay close to the desk all the time, he has an opportunity to seek out prospective clients and visit the old ones. This makes working more efficient and productive while at the same time nurturing customer interests. Automatic observation also helps to reduce operational costs because the same amount of work can be done with fewer employees.

Insurance

Mobility is an integral part of the insurance industry. Insurance professionals spend a substantial amount of time out of the office, meeting customers and estimating damages caused by accidents, fires and vandalism. The salary of most professionals is dependent on the amount of sales, so up-to-date information about customers becomes a critical factor for success. Efficient communication is also necessary to make sales. Channels for clients, suppliers and management have to be open for optimal results.

Using a mobile device, an insurance professional can access corporate information systems regardless of his location. In addition, he has a real-time connection to e-mail and other messaging solutions, enabling a faster response to customer requests. Before going to a customer, he can access information about current products, claims and prior engagements. Using a mobile terminal, the insurance professional can also rate customers and select those with the largest potential. This way, important customers can be offered better customer service and individual treatment. Using a mobile terminal, the sales representative is able to configure quotes and compare the suitability of different products for the customer. Instant price information and counselling helps the representative to close more deals on the spot.

Some other benefits for using a mobile device at the client site are:

- instant claims tracking;
- streamlined business processes (billing, claims adjudication, information updates);
- reduced administrative costs, no retyping;
- productivity increase;
- more efficient resource planning;
- improved data accuracy;
- better facilities to respond to momentum-building, deal-making circumstances.

Logistics and transportation

The logistics and transportation business is becoming more time sensitive as the manufacturing and retail sector require materials to be delivered on time.

At the same time, the management of multiple layered processes makes logistics and transportation increasingly complex. The field is also characterized by fierce competition and decreasing margins. To decrease costs and optimize customer satisfaction, the maximum utilization of a fleet and other resources is needed.

Changing routes, schedules and arrival times make it challenging to keep up efficient communication between the call center and driver. In a traditional situation, the driver contacts the call center several times a day with a voice call in order to receive additional information about destinations, routes and freight. Call centers are often overloaded with multiple processes taking place at the same time. This results in high operational costs, delays, dissatisfied customers and lower utilization of transportation utilities. Additionally, drivers do not have access to important information at their destination resulting in communication blackouts between the customer and the driver. Therefore, a real-time data connection between a driver and a call center is crucial in making transportation more efficient and reliable.

The companies best suited for time-critical data solutions are:

➤ taxis;

➤ suppliers (rentals, office supplies, food delivery…);

➤ heavy transportation;

➤ waste disposal companies;

➤ delivery companies (oil, gas…).

Using a mobile data solution, drivers and call centers share the same information wherever they are. Call centers are no longer overloaded as communication takes place solely between, customers and the company. During the telephone call, a representative types information into a corporate system accessible from mobile terminals. After that, dispatching may take place automatically, without human intervention. Dynamic fleet dispatch can be assigned according to the location of a driver if the trucks are equipped with Global Positioning System (GPS). Otherwise, automatic dispatching may take place based on freight materials or assigned areas of the drivers. However, most companies depend on a special professional dispatcher to assign jobs. The dispatcher sends the assignments to a driver via instant messaging. In return, the driver updates information using his mobile terminal. The dispatcher knows the status of assignments at all times. A mobile data solution helps the dispatcher in scheduling and routing because of increased accuracy in job tracking. She is able to handle more drivers and customer accounts than dispatchers in the traditional model. Faster customer service and more efficient package tracking is possible with fewer resources and operating expenses. The drivers are also able to handle more assignments because of more efficient routing. Because arrival times can be forecast more accurately, freight terminal management and outbound plans can be improved and optimized.

Location-based services have great potential for the transportation industry. They also enhance the security of the drivers because there is always someone who knows the location of the truck, so in an emergency or in case of theft, the location of a truck can be instantly spotted on the map and an ambulance or a police car can be sent to the scene. Another strong point for location-based solution is increased efficiency because of better route planning and the ability to forecast arrival times.

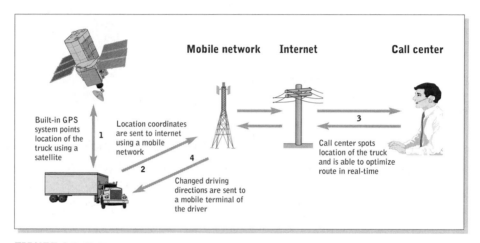

FIGURE 4.8 Dynamic fleet dispatch takes place as the call center knows the location of all vehicles in real-time

Some of the common functions of location-based transportation solutions are:

- vehicle utilization measurement;
- driver performance measurement;
- location-based dispatching;
- dynamic route planing;
- integration with the internet tracking system;
- profit and loss reporting;
- graphical maps for a dispatcher showing location of the drivers;
- driver hours tracking.

Public sector and utility industry

In most countries, competition in utilities and the public sector is facing increasing demands because states, cities and municipalities outsource most of the operations. Companies are under pressure to decrease operational costs, improve customer service and make workers more efficient. The public sector and the utility industry are also characterized by a large number of mobile workers and long distances between departments.

Some of the fields falling into this category are:

➤ electricity;

➤ gas;

➤ municipal distribution;

➤ power and water departments.

Organizations are able to share information dynamically when employees and hardware are connected to each other by mobile technology. Field engineers and mechanics use mobile terminals to enter their working hours into the system. They can also interact with a call center and management to receive emergency notifications and status updates. Some companies use mobile units to monitor hardware such as electricity plants and water machinery. This way, emergency messages can be dynamically dispatched to the closest field engineer. Time-consuming searches for skilled professionals are automatically taken care of by the system that has the skill profiles of all the workers, so machine break-down times can be minimized. The cost saving compared to traditional systems is substantial. At the destination, field engineers are able to order spare parts and access troubleshooting databases with a mobile terminal. Because spare parts ordering and inventory management takes place digitally, paperwork is reduced and administrative costs from retyping and other duplicated processes is cut down. Additionally, the efficiency of the field workers is enhanced because of the automated ordering process and better communication. On the other hand, the management and dispatchers are always aware of the status of the worker and service planning becomes easier. As a result of optimized dispatching, the efficiency of the field engineer increases.

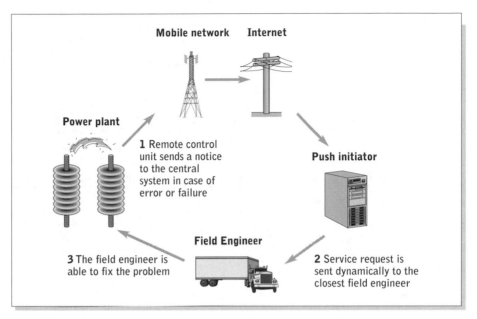

FIGURE 4.9 ■ Automated job dispatch using remote control units at the power plant

Notes and references

1. "Telemetry: Red Hot In Ice Distribution," Wireless Week, www.wirelessweek.com (July 31, 2000).

5

Location-based services

Potential for operators and partners

Mobile operators, financial institutions and content providers are competing to acquire direct customer relationships in mobile commerce. Financial institutions offer payment infrastructure and security. Content providers are strong in entertainment and news. Mobile operators have a direct billing relationship with the customer. The player with superior services will win the game. As operators own mobile networks, they are able to generate additional revenue from value added services.

Network-based location technologies have developed substantially during the past couple of years. This is because the Federal Communications Commission (FCC) requires operators in the US to provide the location of all mobile emergency calls – the market has been government-driven until now. The operators are currently looking for ways to benefit from the massive network investments. European and Asian operators are also looking for ways to provide location-based services. Network infrastructure providers are developing platforms to meet that need. Ericsson, for example, has developed Mobile Position System (MPS), providing an open Application Programmer Interface (API) for third party developers. A toolkit for location-dependent service creation can also be downloaded, free, from their website.

What is the business case for location-based services?

According to research organizations, location-based applications have obvious success potential. Strategy Analytics, for example, believes that location-based services could generate $6 billion of revenue in western Europe by 2005 and $4.6 billion in North America during the same time. More than half of the US customer base is willing to accept some advertising on a mobile handset if they are able to use location services for free.[1]

Finding a business case for location-based services is not difficult. Corporate users benefit from increased efficiency and cost savings when deploying location-sensitive extensions for their existing mobile applications. Fleet management and customer relationship management solutions aim to maximize the use of resources and minimize costs in the dynamic business environment. Dynamic vehicle routing is becoming one of the most successful location-aware corporate solutions because enterprises can see a clear business case for cutting down vehicle maintenance costs and expenses. In addition, customer relationship management benefits from the increased efficiency of field workers as they can be dispatched to the closest client site when needed. Field workers are thus able to handle more customers during the same time period while customer satisfaction increases because of faster service.

The business case for consumer solutions is different from corporate principles. However, companies considering the deployment of location-based consumer applications should develop ROI (Return On Investment) models and business plans. This way, expenses can be estimated and project goals are clear for all participants. An essential part of making a business plan for location sensitive consumer applications is to define possible motives for using the service. Forecasting the popularity of a service that is totally new for consumers is extremely difficult. Identification of motives helps to address the core target groups and segments.

Possible consumer motives for using a location-based service are:

➤ convenience;
➤ motives of belonging and being a part of the group;
➤ saving time;
➤ saving money;
➤ general interest in new things;
➤ recognition.

The business case, is presented in Figure 5.1 below. To begin with, opportunities and limitations of the technology play an important role in location-based services because accuracy and infrastructure requirements vary between different solutions. Push and pull solutions are very different in terms of technology because push basically requires the location of the user to be spotted actively in real-time. Most users of pull solutions update their location only when using the services.

User requirements and suitable applications are defined based on technology. The process is influenced by the business environment because competition in consumer solutions and substitute processes in the corporate environment have a great impact on user adoption.

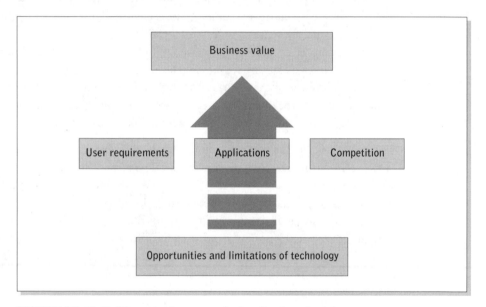

FIGURE 5.1 ■ Building a business case for location-based services

diAx in Switzerland

diAx, the Swiss fixed and mobile operator, offers a variety of location-based services to its WAP customers. The WAP portal from diAx includes a new menu entry, mRegio, that subscribers are able to use to access, among other things, location-based news, weather forecasts, traffic information and events. diAx is cooperating with SignalSoft, a company that provides location technology and telecommunications platform products.

The WAP address of mRegio is http://www.mregio.ch and diAx can be found at http://www.diax.ch using a normal web browser.

FIGURE 5.2 ■ The web page of diAx

Defining target groups and their needs

Users of location-based services can be divided into two main categories: time-savers and money-savers. Time-savers have plenty of money but a limited amount of time. Most corporations fall into this category. They are looking for convenient solutions to make their lives easier and more efficient and are willing to pay for applications that can streamline processes and make their operations more efficient. Money-savers have plenty of time but no money. They are primarily interested in applications that offer subsidies and location-based advertising. In many cases, they are willing to receive advertisements in return for free calls or discount coupons.

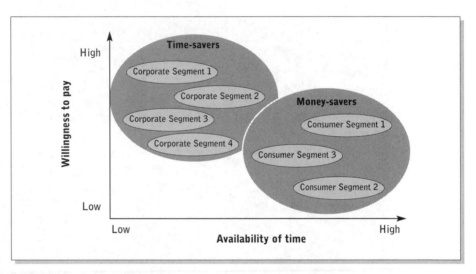

FIGURE 5.3   ■   The target groups of location-based services

Real-time monitoring — push applications

Privacy concerns

Usually, a user subscribes to push services by personalizing the service via the fixed internet. Once she has decided what kind of alerts and messages she wants to receive, the service does not require any additional attention. The network of a mobile operator is constantly aware of the location of the user and the system sends instant messages based on predefined trigger values. For example, when the user is approaching a traffic jam, the system sends her a warning message with an alternative route.

Security and privacy are some of the key issues in location-based push services. In the case of security leaks, third parties would be able to track the location of individuals and use that information for questionable purposes. With little imagination, push applications have the potential to become horror stories of the new technology, where society and organizations track individuals and control their freedom. Companies planning to deploy push applications should follow the development of general opinion closely and make the appropriate moves according to the opinions of users.

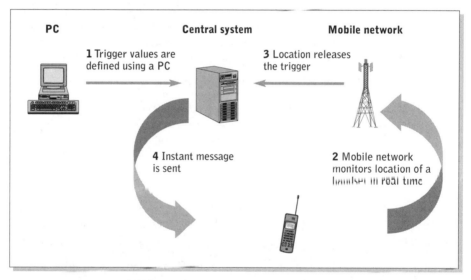

FIGURE 5.4 ■ The challenge of push applications is that the location of the user has to be known at all times. Therefore, retail advertisements and different alert messages (weather and traffic alerts) can be pushed into mobile terminals. This is also a major privacy concern because individual handsets can be spotted

Retail alerts and targeted advertising

Marketing and location-based technologies are a powerful combination, enabling services we can only dream of. As noted earlier, personalization is the key to a successful mobile service. With one-to-one marketing, it is a necessity.

The process of one-to-one marketing would go like this:

1. The customer subscribes to a "product alarm" service using a normal internet connection. Membership is granted after he has given his personal information, together with some details about himself. He lists the following information into the alarm service:

    –   Product: stereos

    –   Price: under 400 USD

    –   Alarm deadline: 2 weeks

    –   Visibility range: 1,000 meters

2. After listing all the details, he activates the service.

3. Now, for a couple of weeks, he is going to be an open target to all parties selling stereos and participating in the advertising service. When he comes within the range of 1,000 meters of a company selling stereos for less than 400 dollars, he may receive a personalized message to his phone, telling him about this amazing opportunity.

Obviously, a service like this requires many parties and the only way of providing this kind of one-to-one marketing concept is to go into partnership with various companies. The service provider would also need an extensive database with geocoded information which would also have to be constantly updated.

Companies that are likely to offer one-to-one marketing are the established "Brick and Mortar" chains that have an extensive number of retail outlets. Service stations could also use one-to-one marketing to notify customers about special gas deals. In addition, franchising companies, like McDonalds, can use one-to-one channels to increase customer loyalty.

Another set of companies likely to offer one-to-one marketing are internet start-ups who act as intermediaries to provide customers with the lowest possible price. These companies, like Realestate.com, could change their business model slightly and start providing their customers with localized offerings from established brands. Some of these intermediaries already have infrastructures and business models in place. The only thing missing is translating the information into a format whereby locations have geographical coordinates.

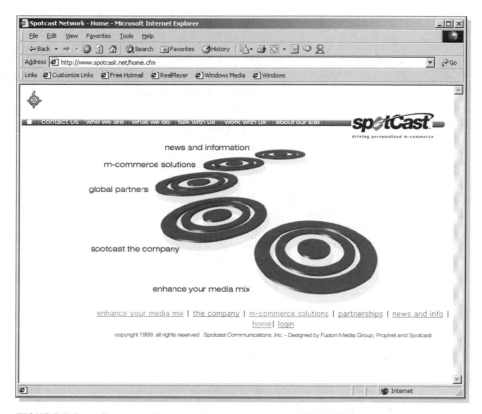

FIGURE 5.5 ■ Spotcast offers precision-targeted advertising campaigns

During the era of e-commerce, marketing professionals have been attracted to the concept of information intermediaries. Intermediaries have an extensive database of customers and they constantly generate more and more information about them. This way, more targeted advertisements can be sent to the customer, resulting in better outcomes for campaigns. In the era of mobile commerce, information intermediaries will become increasingly important. For lower prices, customers are willing to give their personal profiles to the intermediaries. They in turn, are able to provide the customers with information they would not otherwise encounter.

Cell advertising

Cell advertising is yet another approach to mobile advertising solutions. It is technically easier to build than other location-based services because it does not require a very accurate determination of an individual handset. A cell is the geographical area covered by a cellular telephone transmitter. The area of one cell can be from one kilometer to twenty kilometers in diameter, depending on terrain and transmission power. Companies deploying cell advertising are, basically, sending a message to all subscribers who are currently in a particular cell. This way, they are able to reach mobile phone users within a loosely defined area and send them advertising messages. The receivers of cell advertising messages are able to log into their personalized website and personalize the service. That way, they can define, beforehand, particular times or locations that are not suitable for them. In addition, personal interests and product categories can be inserted into the system.

The target group of cell advertising is, naturally, money-savers who have plenty of time. They are looking for great deals and, possibly, some subsidized services in return for receiving the advertisements.

Traffic, weather and gas station alerts

Traffic, weather and gas station alert providers generate their income from instant messages. The subscribers are willing to pay for information if they can avoid traffic jams, hurricanes or missing the last gas station along the highway. Some services are also likely to be sponsored because new advertising concepts will be introduced as the location-based alerts become more popular.

User interface and processes are the main challenges for personalized alert messages. Is it possible to make a service that is so convenient and easy to use that the users recommend it to their friends and neighbors? To include real-time location spotting and changing content calls for special requirements for the network infrastructure and scalability.

Both time and money savers use alert services. Some subscribers are looking for good deals in return for receiving the messages. Others may pay for value added services, e.g. knowing that they will be notified if there is a traffic jam ahead.

Defining an appropriate target group for push services

As described in the beginning of this chapter, there are two main target groups for location-based services: money-savers and time-savers. In push services, the major focus is on consumer solutions offering sponsored content for money-savers. This way, retailers and service companies are able to offer their products directly to consumers when they are physically close to the store or office.

In contrast, systems integrators and corporations are very interested in time-savers because they are willing to pay for content and accurate service. Primarily, companies with special interest in field engineering and transportation are able to build a clear business case for location-based services and custom solutions. Systems integrators have a great chance to offer their back-end knowledge for these projects because they require complex integration of the existing software packages and the new technology.

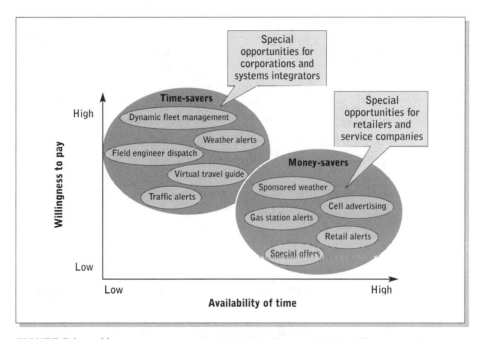

FIGURE 5.6 ■ Money-savers are primarily looking for good deals as Time-savers have plenty of money but a limited amount of time

Location on the spot — pull applications

Pull applications are generally easier to implement than push applications because location of the user is updated only when the services are really needed. Therefore, the mobile network does not have to actively "track" the user and spot his location on a regular basis.

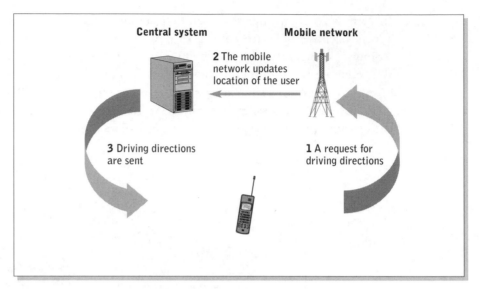

FIGURE 5.7 ■ The process of using pull services

The only exception to the picture above are those pull services that spot the location of other people or vehicles. In these cases, the mobile network can monitor the location of all the parties on regular basis, or the service can be controlled by the users. In a user-controlled solution, instant messages notify the parties and authorize the users.

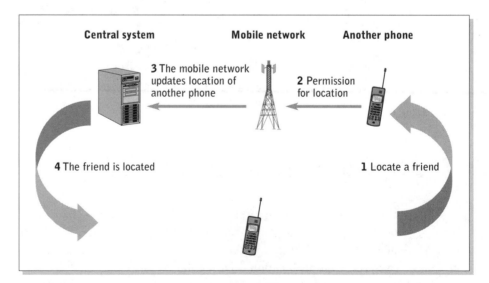

FIGURE 5.8 ■ The process of locating another phone in a user-controlled solution

Locate your friends and family

Location-based entertainment and community services require less collaboration between different providers. Therefore, some of them can be produced by mobile operators wanting to increase customer loyalty by offering exciting premium services. Basically, the service provider offers a framework for the service. The users create the content they want so the operating cost of the service is low while potential revenue expectations are high.

What kind of entertainment and community services are possible with location technology?

1. A group of people decide that they will "see" each others' positions. Therefore, everyone needs to give permission to the other members of the group. Those having permission can request the location of the other members and arrange meetings according to information provided by the service. For example, Jeff is able to see the location of all the members in his family. When they go shopping on Saturday, he can constantly keep up with them and suggest meeting points based on their location. An alarm service is also able to notify him when other people belonging to the same location service and group are close by. Therefore, his mobile handset beeps when Joe Copper, his uncle, is within a radius of 200 meters. Using his mobile phone, Jeff can call him up and arrange a meeting point immediately.

2. A shooting party is going elk hunting. Everyone knows the position of the others based on the location service. After the elk has been shot, the location of the animal can be communicated to everyone. Some members could monitor the hunting situation with their laptop computers and communicate possible safety risks.

3. Amy belongs to the Redwood Stamp Collectors Club. She has agreed to use a location-based community service with her friends. On Friday night, she enters the password-protected website of the group and checks where everybody is hanging out. Using her personal computer, she is able to see a graphical map and the location of all her friends. After a quick look, it seems evident that most of her friends are hanging out at the local McDonalds. Amy sends a short message suggesting a visit to the stamp exhibition not far from there.

For entertainment and community service, the operator has to provide a secure connection between all the participants. In addition, a web interface, together with integrated message capabilities, is useful. It is likely that location-based entertainment and community services will be a killer revenue generator for mobile operators. In addition, they are a way to differentiate mobile operators from each other. Young people, especially, are likely to choose their mobile operator according to the services they are able to offer. If all of their friends are using the location-based community service of a particular mobile operator, it is highly unlikely that someone would choose another operator just for lower prices. The same applies to families and other closely related groups.

⣿ CASE STUDY

CellPoint Finder!

Users of CellPoint Finder! can locate each other and communicate in a new way. They start by choosing a list of friends who they would like to locate or be seen by. When a user wants to see the location of his friend, he may use a computer or a phone interface to request the information. The answer is returned in a form of an address, such as "John is close to Piccadilly Circus, about 3.2 km west of you".

CellPoint markets the solution as a turn-key package with hardware and software installation together with maintenance and upgrades. This way, the operator has to take care of marketing, sales and customer care. Some advantages of the solution are short time-to-market, easy maintenance and large user potential

Emergency and security services

It has been estimated that in Finland, around 40 per cent of all the emergency calls come from mobile phones. How many lives could be saved by providing the location of the caller? Emergency solutions in the US are actually driving the technical development of location-based services. There, mobile operators have to be able to provide the location of the caller. Because of this, all the operators are installing location technology as a part of their network. In the future, location-based emergency services will be an integral part of mobile communication.

Security solutions are targeted to a limited group of people in an occupation or situation where location brings increased security to the individual. Night-watchmen and policemen are able to use location technology for higher security. This way, their current position is always known and, in the case of accidents or emergencies, additional help can be sent directly, without having to determine the location of the person first.

CASE STUDY

Matrix Vehicle Tracking

Matrix Vehicle Tracking has been very successful in tracking stolen vehicles in South Africa. Based on CellPoint's technology, a small GSM transmitter is inserted into the car. In a case of hijacking the transmitter can be activated and positioned. The average time to track down a stolen vehicle is 40 minutes and over 90 per cent of all the stolen cars with the transmitter have been recovered. This translates to over 1,700 vehicles during the past three years.

Yellow pages

In the beginning of the internet, search engines played an important role in offering an easier way to find information – the internet would not be what it is today without search engines. Later on, search engines stretched to cover more services and became portals offering e-mail, calendar and online shopping. This way, former search engines have been able to attract more customers and benefit from their established position. With the emergence of mobile commerce, companies are, obviously, looking for something that could bring long term profits and enable a natural migration path as mobile networks develop. It has been speculated that mobile yellow pages will follow the success of web search engines, or at least play an important role in the mobile portals of the future.

What are the practical solutions offered to customers with mobile yellow pages? These are just some of the ways the customers could use the service:

➤ Find the nearest fast food restaurant, hair dresser, gas station…

➤ Where is the Natural History Museum in London?

➤ How do I get to the closest shopping mall?

➤ Show me all the camping sites within 10 kilometers.

➤ Search the yellow pages with a keyword "baseball". Return all the matches within the radius of three kilometers.

It is possible to generate these kind of services with geocoded yellow page information, location coordinates and maps. These are likely to be some of the first location-based services.

However, yellow page companies should focus on additional information that could give substantial value to consumers. They could generate additional revenue in services where the yellow page information leads directly to a purchase. The following examples require frequently updated databases and more active cooperation between the yellow page company and its partners.

➤ Search all the gas stations within 10 kilometers and return three with the lowest prices.

➤ I want to order a taxi to my current position.

➤ I have a car breakdown. Please locate me and send some help.

➤ Locate the closest restaurants with lunch less than eight dollars.

➤ I want to buy a fishing license for my current position. Please debit my account with the mobile operator.

The providers of yellow pages have massive amounts of information that can be used when providing information for mobile devices. Lately, some yellow page providers on the internet have even started to provide customers with maps showing the location of companies. Naturally, in order to do that, they must know the location coordinates of the company. This enables them to provide mobile location services with a small effort compared to many other companies.

Operators are able to provide the location coordinates of a mobile device. Therefore, the yellow page company should enter into a partnership with the operator and agree on revenue sharing deals. If the operator has an established mobile portal, the mobile yellow pages should be integrated into the portal to attract more customers. Additionally, customer privacy should be guaranteed because security leaks in an area like this would be fatal to the service.

CASE STUDY

Go2 Systems

Go2 Systems have developed a service called Go2 NetGates which delivers proximity-based listings for more than 11 million stores and destinations. The service is based on WAP standard and it can be used with any WAP-capable phone. The ultimate goal of the company is to provide smart phone users with a variety of location-based merchant information such as specials and parking place details. Initially, the information will be based on area ZIP codes.

SignalSoft Local.info

Local.info is an application from SignalSoft combining location with content. Personalized, real-time information about local entertainment, traffic and roadside assistance can be provided. In addition, a variety of internet and e-commerce content can be added. The service can be accessed via WAP, voice recordings, short messages or call centers.

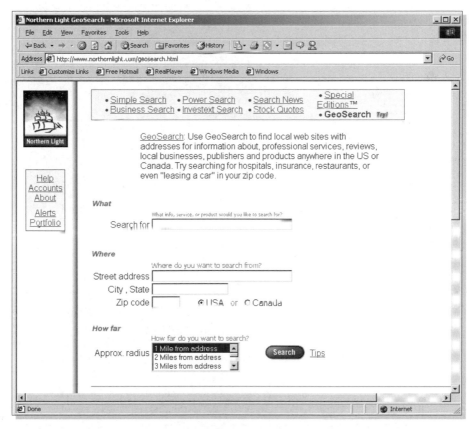

FIGURE 5.9 ■ Northern Light has established a service where the search engine can be used to find places according to user's location

Defining a target group for pull applications

Both money-savers and time-savers are interested in location-based pull applications. Depending on the business model of the service provider, the same applications can be targeted at both segments. For example, driving directions are primarily offered to time-savers, but sponsored driving directions would interest money-savers as well. Therefore, sponsorship and different subsidized services (free voice calls, discount coupons) are likely to attract a large horizontal audience.

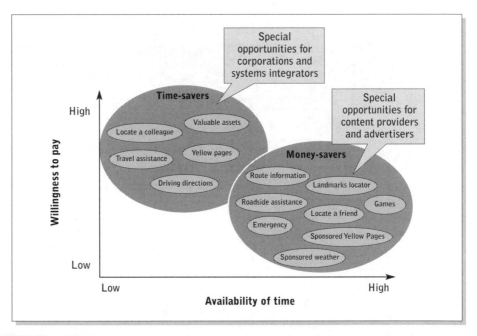

FIGURE 5.10 ■ Target segments for location-based pull applications. Corporations are primarily looking for increased efficiency because the same tasks can be handled with fewer resources and time (time-savers). In contrast, consumers are interested in services that help them save money or offer sponsored value added applications (money-savers)

Moving away from wired telephones

Zonal billing

Basically, there are two types of operators offering mobile services:

➤ traditional operators with a mobile department; and

➤ operators who specialize in mobile services alone.

The latter are more interested in zonal billing because, this way, they are able to replace the use of wired phones. With zonal billing, the mobile operator defines where the calls are substantially cheaper. Usually, this cell is located where mobile phone usage is the highest. Therefore, "home cells" could be the offices or homes of individuals. The tendency to move from wired phones to mobile phones can already be seen in Nordic European countries (Norway, Sweden, Finland) with mobile phone penetration of 50-70 per cent. There, location-based billing would probably lead to companies with no wired phones.

According to Luton-based Strategy Analytics, 40 per cent of wireless phone users in Europe will stop using fixed telephones for voice calls over the next decade. The development is lead by the 16-to-24-year-old group which has significantly higher usage levels for services such as short messages and e-mail.[2]

Technology for location-based services

There are two ways to determine the location of a handset: a network-based solution by a mobile operator and a handset-based solution, usually done by attaching a GPS receiver to a mobile phone or installing a special piece of software into a SIM card. In most cases, the mobile network is actively used when offering location-based services. With handset-based solutions, the operator can be passed because the location is determined according to the handset information. The value chains of the different technologies are slightly different.

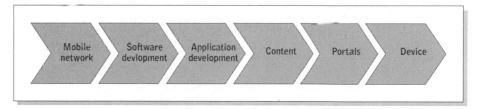

FIGURE 5.11 ■ Value chain of a network-based solution

In a network-based solution, coordinates are determined in the network where special software components calculate the location of a handset. Additionally, a piece of software may be needed in the mobile phone for increased accuracy.

Therefore, a mobile network is the first stop on the way to creating a location-based service. After that, software and application development takes place in order to design a special piece of software capable of retrieving information from the network and managing user sessions. Continually, the piece of software integrates content and location coordinates together and passes the processed information on to a mobile handset. Mobile portals can be used to offer consumers a single entry point for various applications, including location-based services.

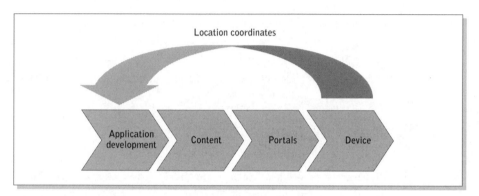

FIGURE 5.12 ■ Value chain of a handset-based solution

The value chain of a handset-based solution is slightly different because mobile operators are passed and they are used merely as facilitators rather than application providers. This enables other parties to provide location services without sharing the revenue with operators.

There are three ways to offer operator-independent location services:

➤ a special piece of software is embedded into a mobile device operating system or into a SIM card;

➤ combined mobile phone and GPS receiver (Finnish mobile phone manufacturer, Benefon, already has this kind of model);

➤ fixed car navigation system with a GPS unit, exclusively for providing telemetry services.

Except for car navigation systems, the market forecast for handset-based location-services is not the best, unless device manufacturers take a more aggressive role in providing handsets with location capabilities. Mobile operators are able to use their existing distribution channels for providing network-based location services and in the future they are likely to be very strong.

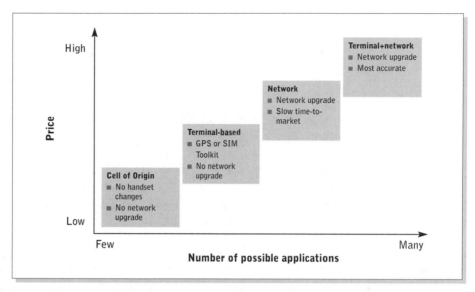

FIGURE 5.13 ■ Location technologies based on price and number of possible applications

Cell of Origin

The Cell of Origin is the simplest way to provide the location of a subscriber. The network operator knows in what cell the caller is located. The accuracy is dependent on the density of the cell-sites or base stations. Therefore, cities, where most of the location-based services are used, have higher accuracy than rural areas. Response time is relatively fast, approximately three seconds, and the accuracy varies from 150 meters in high density pico-cell areas to 30 kilometers in rural areas. 3G networks are able to determine the location of an individual handset more accurately because the cells are smaller to achieve increased bandwidth.

Location-dependent services (in urban areas) based on Cell of Origin could be, for example:

> weather news and alerts;

> friend/family member location;

> stolen car tracking;

> cell broadcast for personalized advertisement/red alert;

> traffic reports/alerts.

The services that are based on the Cell of Origin do not require upgrades to the existing networks or mobile handsets. Therefore, the time-to-market is very fast.

Terminal-based

There are three ways to determine the location of a handset when using terminal-based solutions:

➤ GPS (Global Positioning System);

➤ software residing on a SIM card with phones supporting SIM Toolkit;

➤ software residing in the mobile terminal.

The Global Positioning System is controlled and financed by the US Department of Defense. GPS receivers calculate their location based on operational GPS satellites moving at 1.8 miles per second. Between five and eight satellites are visible from any point on earth.

GPS is an accurate way to determine the location of a handset. The accuracy does not depend on the density of network base stations, so the location can be determined with an accuracy of 100 meters or less horizontally and 156 meters vertically in both urban and rural areas. The problems of GPS are high battery consumption and speed – sometimes, the response time can take up to one minute. In addition, GPS can only be used outside, in the open air. Therefore, use in urban areas is likely to remain low because tunnels and buildings block visibility. High price and other requirements such as size and design decrease the device manufacturers' interest in making GPS a standard functionality for mobile phones. It will be used primarily in fixed objects, such as cars, boats and shipments, to provide services with high accuracy.

Possible applications for GPS-based solutions are:

➤ emergency services (boat, snowmobile in a storm);

➤ guiding/finding applications for cars;

➤ points of interest along the driving route;

➤ shipment and fleet tracking;

➤ stolen car tracking;

➤ traffic information/alerts;

➤ mobile yellow pages for vehicles.

Another option for handset-based location services is to deploy software inside a mobile terminal. It may reside on a SIM card that can be inserted into a phone that supports SIM Toolkit, or inside the phone, installed by a device manufacturer. Both of the solutions calculate the location of a handset using mobile networks, so the density of the base stations affects accuracy. In urban areas accuracy is better than in rural areas because the base stations are closer to each other.

CASE STUDY

CellPoint

CellPoint is a company providing a software-based location solution for GSM operators. The solution uses SIM Application Toolkit-enabled mobile phones which are equipped with a new SIM card. The CellPoint system does not require any updates to a mobile network because it is completely handset-based. Accuracy depends on the density of the base stations, normally ranging from 50 to 200 meters in urban areas. Users do not have to buy new handsets if the existing device supports the SIM Application Toolkit. Only the SIM card of the existing handset has to be changed. Therefore, the initial investment is low and operators are able to launch new location-based services very fast.

Some of the applications of CellPoint are:

➤ personal safety and emergency assistance;

➤ resource management service;

➤ information service (yellow pages);

➤ CellPoint Finder!™ (a friend locator).

Network

Network-based solutions use various techniques to determine the location of the handset. However, network based solutions require an upgrade to the existing network and are, therefore, more expensive for operators than technologies based on a SIM Toolkit or Cell of Origin. Currently, network-dependent solutions provide an accuracy ranging from 100 to 200 meters. However, network infrastructure providers are developing techniques that could increase the accuracy with future network technology.

Infrastructure providers are developing intelligent network solutions where the location of a handset can easily be specified and that information could be passed on to third party developers. The architectural component is called

Mobile Location Center (MLC) and it provides parties with an open Application Programmer Interface (API). APIs are used to enable third party developers to engage in partnerships with network operators and develop applications using the geographical coordinates of individual handsets.

Terminal and network-based solutions

The solutions requiring modifications to both the network and the terminal are the slowest to market but may provide increased accuracy. Network assisted GPS, for example, is used for high accuracy in both rural and urban areas. With GPS, the same problems exist regarding size, response time and battery life. Therefore, network assisted GPS is likely to be used in fixed objects like cars and shipments, where size and battery consumption are not a problem. It could be used to locate taxi drivers, valuable assets, shipments, trains and special units of police forces.

CASE STUDY

SnapTrac

SnapTrack from San Jose is a pioneer in network aided GPS solutions. The company is now owned by Qualcomm and, therefore, it is likely that their technology will be embedded into Qualcomm CDMA chips. With network assisted GPS, SnapTrack is able to locate a handset within 5 to 20 meters. Therefore, the technology may be used with, literally, all imaginable location-based services. The software also enables the user to deactivate the service and offers, therefore, increased privacy. NTT DoCoMo, the biggest mobile operator of packet switched data services, is using SnapTrack for their DocoNavi Personal Location Service.

CASE STUDY

Cambridge Positioning System (CPS)

Cambridge Positioning System (CPS) is developing a solution based on a special piece of software integrated into a mobile phone. With the CPS solution, called Cursor, a handset can usually be located with an accuracy of 125 meters. In ideal circumstances, the accuracy of a Cursor system may rise to 25 meters. The response time is approximately five seconds. Cursor has entered a deal with Phillips Semiconductor in order to get the software embedded in Phillips chips. Therefore, Mitsubishi is likely to use Cursor technology in their handsets. In addition, CPS is negotiating with several other device manufacturers to get their software embedded into their terminals. The use of Cursor requires a network upgrade and special equipment at the base stations.

What is the best strategy?

Without a doubt, location-based services have great potential to become the killer applications of mobile commerce. However, mobile operators are taking various routes in approaching the new technology. The following table presents some of the options:

TABLE 5.1 ■ Various approaches to location-based services

	Aggressive approach	Conservative approach
Service launch	Immediate. Begin with less accurate technology solutions and experiment with user adoption.	Wait. See how aggressive operators succeed in their ventures.
Technology	Deploy Cell of Origin initially. Begin with solutions which have a short time to market. Pull applications, such as weather forecasts, are an easy way to begin because location of the user is updated only when he uses the service. Introduce push applications such as traffic alerts later on because they require location of the user to be known all the time. Proceed to applications requiring high accuracy as soon as enabling technology becomes available.	Wait for out-of-the-box solutions from network infrastructure providers and device manufacturers.
Position in the value chain	Aggressively develop and deploy location-based technology. Start product development with selected partners. Intend to offer out-of-the-box solutions for other operators.	Concentrate on your core competency. Outsource everything else.

	Aggressive approach	Conservative approach
Partnerships	Partner with location technology providers. Intend to engage in joint ventures and testing in order to stay ahead of your competitors.	Partner with operators that have already deployed location-based services. Learn from their mistakes.
Risks	Manage risks by acquiring personnel with strong technology capabilities. Predict the future by cooperating with companies that provide location technology.	Manage risks by waiting and participating in forums in order to become aware of development.
Competition	Be first in the market. Use this position for building a strong brand. Get to know your customers.	Learn from the mistakes of the early movers. Develop services with proven concepts.
Marketing	Market the services aggressively. Try to build an innovative and customer-oriented brand.	Launch massive campaigns for services with proven concepts.
Vertical vs. horizontal markets	Use vertical markets (security, resource management) in order to experiment with the service. Learn from your mistakes and move on to horizontal markets with large volumes.	Wait until you have enough information on the horizontal markets. Concentrate on simple services with low initial investments.

In addition, content providers, systems integrators and application developers should take some action to position themselves correctly regarding new location-based services. What would be the best approach to gain additional knowledge of such services and develop the expertise needed for their deployment?

TABLE 5.2 ■ Acquiring the necessary information

	Content provider	Systems integrator	Application developer
Partnership	Engage in partnerships with mobile operators in order to have access to the location information of their subscribers. Find sponsors for your content to offer free services to consumers. Example: "This is a free traffic alert bought to you by Audi".	Form joint ventures with portals and location technology providers.	Form joint ventures with mobile operators in order to get exclusive deals for location-based service development.

	Content provider	Systems integrator	Application developer
Knowledge development	Create an efficient feedback mechanism in order to understand your customers.	Partner with operators in order to understand the requirements for position technology. Start pilot projects with location technology providers to learn the technical requirements for deployment.	Acquire knowledge of security, netcentric development and location technologies. Learn the requirements for location-based technologies in terms of network architecture.
Technical infra-structure	Develop a system for third party advertisers if your business model supports sponsored content. Additionally, focus on personalization and content management technologies.	Learn the basics of network technologies. Create portal platforms integrating traditional mobile applications with location technology.	Develop applications for current terminals which are basically WAP and SMS enabled. Build a scalable server architecture with WAP and SMS gateways.
Position in the value chain	Aim to become an information intermediary of mobile commerce. Create services, where massive amounts of information can be collected from customers.	Shift from basic systems integration towards application development. Focus on location-based mobile commerce and platform development.	Create proprietary solutions that can be licensed around the world. Focus on fast time-to-market.
Market strategies	There are basically two options to choose: ▪ Partner with a strong mobile portal provider in order to reach more customers. ▪ Develop your own mobile portal. Focus on handset-based solutions unless you have access to network-based location information.	Create knowledge on location technology deployment. Use first mover advantage in order to control the market. Become a value added reseller of the leading position technology solution.	Enter the market in partnership with a mobile operator. After developing proprietary solutions, expand operations to cover additional countries. Learn from your mistakes and educate future clients about market characteristics.

	Content provider	Systems integrator	Application developer
Revenue model	Revenue comes from the subscribers of the service and advertisers. In order to increase the revenue from advertisements, personalization technology has to be used. Revenue sharing deals between content providers and mobile operators may be necessary.	Create secure revenue from billable work. In addition, enter into value based billing deals with operators to share the revenue from new services.	Generate revenue from licenses and value based billing, where operator revenue from location-based services is shared according to an agreed-upon deal.
Vertical markets	Localized content for certain business professionals may be created. However, revenues may remain low.	Focus on transportation, customer relationship management and security in order to generate revenue from systems integration. Acquire knowledge of the back-end systems in these areas.	Create simple, fast time-to-market solutions for security and transportation companies.
Horizontal markets	Concentrate on consumer services with volume potential.	Focus on mobile portal platforms integrating location technology with other mass market applications.	Concentrate on consumer services with volume potential.

Notes and references

1. Brad Smith, "France, Japan Differ On Location Strategies," Wireless Week, www.wirelessweek.com (June 26, 2000).

2. Paul Quigley, "Wireless Marketers Need Touch Of Grey," Wireless Week, www.wirelessweek.com (June 19, 2000)

6

Portals

A single plate for various dishes

Portals have become powerful magnets to the internet, attracting millions of customers every day. Some of the early directories and search engines such as Yahoo!, America Online and Altavista are now fully fledged service centers, offering e-mail, news, shopping and dozens of other services. The key concern for portal owners is customer loyalty, also called "stickiness". By offering a large variety of services, portal owners try to keep customers within their site to generate more revenue from advertising and shopping.

Mobile operators, content providers, financial institutions and many others are establishing mobile portal services in order to attract an audience and protect their interests. As discussed in the chapter about the value chain of mobile commerce, markets are still developing and the players seek new positions in the value chain in order to avoid disintermediation. The explosion of a number of internet capable mobile terminals has caused turmoil in mobile markets because the parties are looking for business opportunities and proven models for successful commerce. Numerous mergers and acquisitions take place as companies acquire competitors and escalate their know-how to get better control of the emerging markets.

Several players are entering into the portal business because of its high revenue expectations. According to Ovum, global revenues for wireless portals will reach $42 billion in 2005. This is compared to $747 million in 2000.

Initially, the growth will be smaller but it will accelerate when wireless operators introduce third generation mobile networks. Advertising, e-commerce, content subscriptions and placement fees for portal vendors will account for about $17 billion in 2005.[1]

Portal types

Portal services can be categorized according to different applications. Each service has its strengths and weaknesses, slightly different revenue models and target groups. However, portal services are only categorized to get a better picture of issues affecting business and revenue model. Actual mobile portals should combine the pieces and create a mixture of applications that answer the needs of the customer. Let's take a look at the different types of mobile portals.

Horizontal

Horizontal portals have a mass-market approach and provide information using a wide array of generic applications. In the beginning of mobile commerce, horizontal portals stretch to attract masses because they are trying to build a critical mass needed for market domination. The portals are usually built by big national or international companies with economies of scale. Because it is horizontal, the service has good potential of becoming a market place for mobile commerce later on, when the end terminals enable a wider spectrum of features.

However, horizontal portals, attracting people with different backgrounds and interests, are quite faceless, with general content like news, entertainment and search capabilities. Without real value to the user, horizontal portals are not able to compete against the differentiated services of the market. Over time, they are in danger of losing customers if they fail to generate new, innovative services. Horizontal portal services can choose several strategic options. Some portals may obtain vertical content by buying smaller vertical portals. The new content should be integrated into the existing services seamlessly to maintain a consistent brand image. The vertical content could be sports, financial news or some other, quite generic information. This way, the horizontal portal can start to expand into vertical markets and create customer loyalty by providing communities of interest.

Another way to move into a direction of vertical content is efficient content management. With structured content management, users would be able to create their personal profiles for the service and access specific topics of interest. The content itself can be bought externally from third party aggregators or originators. Horizontal portals should offer personalization because the wealth of information available cannot be accessed conveniently with a small screen mobile terminal without customizing the user interface. Personalization technology is crucial and inevitable.

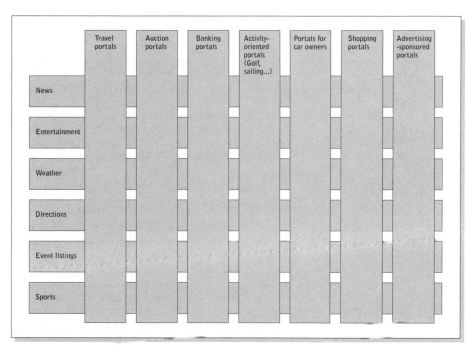

FIGURE 6.1 ■ Horizontal information is meant for everyone. Vertical portals target special interest groups

Another way to improve customer experience and generate additional revenue is location technology. A massive amount of information can be localized for easier customer interface. Location-based advertising becomes possible. Obviously, personalization technology is needed at this point because customers must be able to define what kind of ads they are interested in. Location-based services could be used to create a search engine with location-sensitive conditions.

Horizontal portals embrace the concept "something for everyone". This is both their strength and their biggest weakness. Without personalization, it is extremely hard to deploy targeted advertising because of people's diverse interests and backgrounds. Some of the revenue of the horizontal portals comes from increased air time and some from the combination of mobile commerce and location-based value added services. The service providers should enter into revenue sharing agreements with mobile operators to generate income.

TABLE 6.1 ■ Improving the customer experience

Feature	Implications	Development strategies
Mass-market approach and generic applications	Ability to test the market and see what services customers are interested in.	Monitor the use of applications closely. Compare the revenue streams and production costs of different applications.
Partners and third party content	Content management and real-time connections among the parties become crucial. Revenue sharing agreements.	Engage in partnerships which provide vertical community services. This way, the customer loyalty and "stickiness" is increased.
Distinct users	Everybody wants to have content they are interested in.	Deploy personalized mobile environment where user interface is customizable.
Neutral and vacant	Customer loyalty is a challenge.	Deploy location-based services delivering value added content to the user. Additionally, provide customers with personal communication tools, like e-mail, in order to drive day-to-day use.
Revenue from increased air time, mobile commerce and value added services	Customers are not willing to pay for generic content.	Differentiate. Create vertical communities with premium services. Use location and personalization technology actively for new, value added services. Deploy location-based advertising.

Vertical

Vertical portals target special interest groups and communities – their users are typically like-minded. Examples of vertical portals on the internet are stock brokerage sites (E*Trade) and travel portals (Preview Travel). Additionally, there are portals for corporate customers (such as Industry.net) providing communication tools among parties.

The content of vertical portals is crucial to the customers. Because they are interested in same things, the users do not require special personalization opportunities like the users of horizontal portals. Additionally, location-sensitivity may not be as important as with the horizontal approach. The user of a financial portal does not demand the information to be location-aware because, simply, it does not bring any added value to the user experience. In contrast, the importance of time sensitivity increases and the user is likely to be willing to pay a premium charge for getting the financial news directly to her mobile phone as soon as it hits the market. Therefore, the vertical portals are able to generate additional revenue from premium real-time services.

Vertical portals are basically communities for like-minded people – customer loyalty is high and advertisers are able to focus their message better. Vertical portals are also able to deploy niche applications, delivering more value to the customer. A financial portal could provide access to my bank account, insurance contracts and salary information. This way, the provider of the service can offer a differentiated service resulting in increased customer loyalty. Additionally, time sensitive alert messages can be offered with a premium fee.

▣▣ CASE STUDY

Expedia.com

Online travel portal Expedia.com has developed its Expedia To Go initiative to deliver travel information to handheld computers and mobile devices. Customers of Expedia.com are now able to access frequent flyer account numbers, itineraries, alternative flight schedules, flight status, hotel availability and maps using their mobile phones and PDAs.

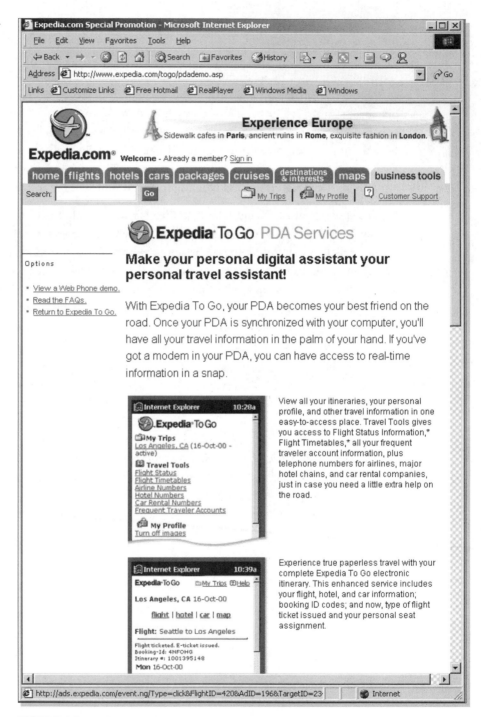

FIGURE 6.2 ■ Expedia.com

TABLE 6.2 ■ Features of vertical portals

Feature	Implications	Development strategies
Highly specialized	Cannot target as wide audience as the horizontal portals.	Create value added services with instant messaging, personalization or location technology in order to generate higher ARPU (Average Revenue Per User).
Social communities	Customer loyalty is high.	Increase customer loyalty even further by providing communication tools (e-mail, chat) for users.
Small producers	Limited resources.	Focus on customer experience. Examine carefully what customers really want. Use your flexibility to answer changing customer expectations.
Attraction of niche markets	Targeted mobile commerce could be deployed.	Offer products and services integrated with content.
Revenue from specialized content, increased air time and premium services	With a small subscriber base, the producer cannot generate substantial revenue.	To increase the subscriber base, you have many options: ■ Partner with horizontal portals to attract new customers ■ Use a multichannel approach by advertising the service in media where potential customers can be reached (American car portal would choose a magazine specializing in American cars) ■ Create affiliate concepts where similar sites cooperate in order to generate more customers

Over time, vertical portals may be swallowed by horizontal players wanting to increase their customer loyalty by providing community services. As they are produced by small companies, vertical portals with steady growth are an interesting option for big, horizontal producers. By buying vertical content, horizontal portals could overcome their lack of customer loyalty.

The revenue model of vertical portals changes case by case. In some cases, revenue is generated through premium services offering real-time instant messaging and access to additional information. Some services, which have an agreement with the operator, rely on the increased air time. Additionally, there are vertical portals aiming to generate their income from targeted advertising and mobile commerce with items relevant to the content of the site.

Multichannel

Multichannel portals combine the benefits of different media and improve the limitations of the mobile channel. A multichannel approach has already been discussed in Chapter 3 about mobile commerce where companies are encouraged to take this approach if their products are not directly suitable for mobile commerce. Print, TV, radio or the fixed internet interface can be combined with a mobile channel to overcome the limitations of screen size and text input. The same channels can also be used for customer acquisition because direct advertisement in the mobile environment may not be very efficient.

An internet portal site and the mobile channel is definitely a strong combination. A mobile portal can be customized using a PC interface and the same e-mail services and other communication tools can be made accessible from both channels. This way, the user can check his e-mail regardless of time and location. Additionally, he may use the most convenient channel in different situations, benefiting from an easy text input and a wider screen while using a PC connection and enjoying the location-independence and time sensitivity of the mobile terminal. The traditional website may also create value added services

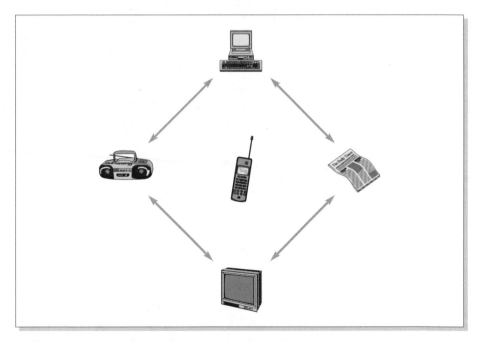

FIGURE 6.3 ■ A multichannel approach for mobile commerce combines TV, radio, print and the fixed internet

based on instant messaging and location technology. This way, the content of the web portal is reused to generate value added services for the customer. For an example, a certain community of members (games, music, sports) may contact each other using a mobile chat service based on location technology. Additionally, the search engine of the PC portal could provide location-dependent search results when using a mobile channel.

The local newspaper is able to deploy a multichannel approach to offer subscribers daily ads in a mobile format. This way, they can access the daily offerings as long as they have a mobile terminal with them. Before heading home from work, locals could get online with their mobile phones and check the discounts at a grocery store. The service could be produced without any special technology (location, personalization) because information is local and time sensitive by default.

Television stations are also able to provide multidimensional, interactive and time sensitive value added services to mobile users. By providing viewers with a reminder via instant messaging when their favorite TV show starts, television stations would, at the same time, acquire information about the preferences of customers and create customer loyalty. Consecutively, television advertisers could have an additional channel for their message. TV ads can be used to promote immediate online transactions. By sending a message to a certain number, the viewer is able to order online settings for her mobile phone. By activating the settings she can access the advertised product directly and make a purchase. As they are characterized by impulsive use, mobile terminals are likely to be used for providing an interactive channel for television advertisers and finalizing the transactions for products advertised on television.

Radio channels can use the mobile environment to reuse content and convert it into a value added service. Additionally, a mobile channel is a way for listeners to participate in programs and provide information in cases where the content is based on interaction. In traffic related programs, listeners could participate by sending real-time traffic comments to the service. Additionally, other listeners could subscribe to a service where they receive the messages, sent by the other drivers, on their mobile terminal. The messages would be location-based and, therefore, relevant to the user. In this case, the radio station acts as an intermediary between the listeners.

As seen in the previous examples, a multichannel approach enables numerous revenue generating services and can overcome the limitations of screen size and text input. The key to success is to embrace the natural characteristics of a mobile device: time sensitivity, location independence, personal manner and impulsive use.

TABLE 6.3 ■ A multichannel approach

Feature	Implications	Development strategies
Multichannel approach in general	■ Strong potential for mobile commerce ■ Improves the limitations of mobile terminals ■ Deploys the strengths and core competencies of existing media ■ Uses the time sensitivity, location independence, personal manner and impulsive use of mobile terminals	See the development strategies defined below.
Fixed internet	■ Customizable mobile interface ■ Lengthy forms can be filled more easily ■ Instant messaging for value added services ■ Combined commerce: see the product online, buy using a mobile phone. ■ E-mail anywhere, anytime ■ The search engine of the web portal transforms into location-based search engine for mobiles	Existing internet portals have to seek partnerships with mobile operators in order to agree on revenue sharing from increased air time. Additionally, mobile operators are able to provide the location of the user. The partnerships should be based on win-win situations, where both of the parties are able to provide additional value to the service.
Print	■ Location-based services without location technology ■ Time sensitive ads ■ Competitions ■ Customer feedback	The print media – magazines and newspapers – should innovate new concepts for increased customer interaction and value added services. By using their core competencies, print media is able to provide services no other player in the value chain is able to offer.
Television	■ Time sensitive instant messaging ■ Ads based on the impulse action of the viewers: "see on TV, purchase online". ■ Customer feedback	TV stations should build secure online market places for advertisers choosing a multi-channel approach. This way, they could promote the new concept and experiment to find the best practices. Additionally, they should enter into agreements with mobile operators in order to offer time sensitive instant messaging.

Feature	Implications	Development strategies
Radio	▪ Reuse of content by packaging it again in a mobile format ▪ Value added services for mobile listeners ▪ A channel for customer interaction ▪ Easily integrated mobile advertising ▪ Time sensitive, location-based services ▪ A natural channel to market music, in the future	Radio stations should seek partnerships. Providing technical platforms for the new services. They should be able to concentrate on their core competence – program production – while the partners would take care of the new technology.

Corporate

Corporate mobile portals are established to benefit from the real-time connectivity and location independence of mobile devices. Some services have been there for a long time with a laptop user interface. However, the new mobile networks and devices are able to offer improved service with instant messaging and faster connectivity. Many companies prefer to place servers providing mobile information inside the company firewall for increased security. This is possible with the new technologies, like WAP, where the mobile operator can be used as a facilitator rather than as a service provider.

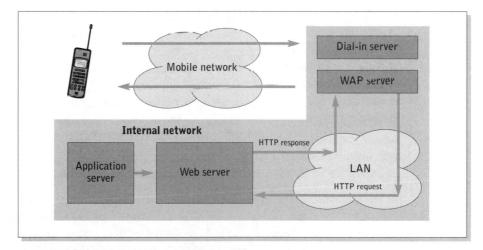

FIGURE 6.4 ▪ Total corporate deployment option. Company has an internal WAP gateway and employees call directly to corporate dial-in server

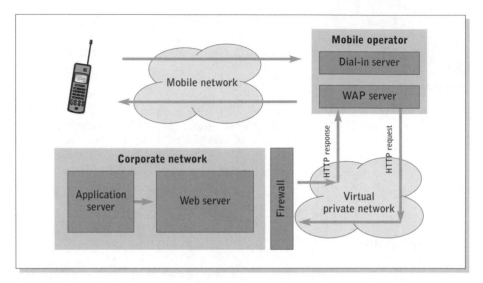

FIGURE 6.5 ■ Outsourced WAP and dial-in server. Corporate data is protected with Virtual Private Network between the firewall and operator network

Applications based on remote control and telematics will be an important part of corporate portals. Coke and copy machines, refrigerators and cars will be able to continually monitor their own status and report malfunctions to a central supervisory system or to the mobile phones of maintenance personnel. Because the price of a transmission chipset goes down all the time, companies are looking for ways to generate cost savings by using the mobile network instead of the public switched telephone network. The mobile transmission chipset enables costly remote units, such as vending machines, to be continually online. Their status can be monitored continually while maintenance and service cost is cut down. Cars are another strong market for the telematics industry. Corporations are able to monitor the status of their fleet at all times and forecast possible defects beforehand. Additionally, quite a few location-based services can be offered for corporate users. Basically, there are two main reasons to use location-based applications in a corporate environment: security and efficiency. Fleet, asset and cargo tracking are used primarily for increased efficiency and better predictability. In cases of emergency and theft, the same tools are able to offer valuable information dynamically.

Mobile customer relationship management (CRM) is another application suited for corporate portals. A mobile sales force may receive new assignments directly to their terminals regardless of their location. In addition to assignment description and information about the customer, the salesperson is also able to drill down into additional information.

For example, the following information may be provided:

> contacts;

> activities;

> personalized customer list;

> customer addresses;

> assignment history;

> team calendar;

> to-do list;

> time reporting.

Mobile customer relationship management is used to increase efficiency and lower communications costs. Additionally, mobile CRM is used to increase customer satisfaction because sales representatives have up-to-date information about their customers. Sales forecasting is also easier because information is updated constantly from the field.

Corporate portals can also benefit from the various applications built especially for the needs of a particular company. Recruitment professionals may use a mobile channel to be updated when suitable applications enter into the system. An instant message is sent to the mobile terminal of a recruitment professional when an application, matching predefined criteria, hits the database. Recruitment professionals are better able to respond to applications and applicant requests without having to be in the office all the time.

Mobile travel reservations, salary information and different team communication solutions are also suitable for a corporate portal environment. Communication solutions are discussed in detail in the next chapter.

TABLE 6.4 ■ Benefits of corporate portals

Applications	Functionality	Development strategies
Mobile Enterprise Resource Planning (ERP)	■ Order entry and inventory status check ■ Order tracking for customers ■ Management reporting	Develop back-end systems in cooperation with a systems integrator. Focus on usability because the limitations of mobile terminals, small screen and limited text input, require special attention.

➤ Applications	Functionality	Development strategies
Machine-to-machine connectivity	▪ Status updates ▪ Malfunction reports	Use mobile transmission chipsets to provide critical information about the machine. Tailored solutions are built by the companies specializing in electronics.
Machine-to-person and person-to-machine connectivity	▪ Malfunction reports ▪ Additional information about the malfunction ▪ Instant troubleshooting and fix	Partner with electronic consulting and software companies to build the interface between the machine and a mobile terminal. Keep in mind that mobile systems may be used for payment processing in the future. Start to build expertise for that now to get a head start over the competitors.
Location-based corporate applications	▪ Fleet management and tracking ▪ Location-based sales force dispatch ▪ Cargo and asset tracking	Combine CRM software with location technology to enable location-based dispatch of field personnel. Develop expertise for cargo and fleet tracking with selected partners.
Mobile Customer Relationship Management (CRM)	▪ Sales force dispatch ▪ Assignment history ▪ Customer information ▪ Real-time quotes at the client site ▪ Communication and team working tools	Examine out-of-the-box solutions for your current CRM software. Develop partnerships with systems integrators in order to learn about the possibilities of mobile CRM.
Tailored solutions	▪ Recruitment ▪ Travel reservations and approval ▪ Salary information	Partner with systems integrators to learn how much effort it would take to build some of the applications.

Communication-oriented

Communication-oriented mobile portals introduce tools already known from the fixed internet. The tools, like e-mail and calendars, are the ones we have been using for the past few years with great satisfaction. E-mail has been the most successful application on the internet, so mobile e-mail has the potential to become a killer application during the era of wireless communication.

Mobile phones, designed initially for voice communication, are now stretching to cover textual communication as well. Text messages have been enormously successful. Finns, for example, sent over a billion text messages during the year 2000. Every text message costs approximately 15 cents. Finland has a population of 5 million. Assuming that they will follow the same pattern, can you imagine what kind of revenue you can make in countries like the US and Germany? SMS messages and other forms of instant messaging are likely to be used actively in the future, because they are perfectly suited for environments with small screens and limited character input.

Mobile portals will also introduce online calendars. Typically, mobile devices already have calendars built in, and, therefore, the success of a portal calendar is not guaranteed. Why would you go online and pay for it if you are able to use the same tool offline for free? Online calendars can be used by other people as well. Therefore, communities and corporations with a lot of team work may use the calendars provided by the mobile portals. This way, the team leader is able to check free space from everybody's calendar while booking a new meeting. Additionally, she can enter the date of a new meeting on the calendar and send an instant message directly to the other members.

Another tool for communication-oriented mobile portals is unified messaging. A unified messaging system combines the different communications media (voice mail, e-mail, instant messaging, fax) into one interface. Ideally, customers can be offered one single service that they can access independently from various channels. Practically, this means that business professionals and consumers could "listen to" their e-mail from any telephone and "read" voice messages using the internet. The key technologies of unified messaging are text-to-speech and speech-to-text applications.

Communication-oriented portals may also offer vertical community services, providing ways of communication for people interested in similar things. People from different age groups have very different needs and expectations regarding content. Therefore, several communities should be established according to the users. Mobile chat and bulletin boards are some of the applications that can be used to generate services. Teenagers can use mobile chat as an extension of fixed internet chatting. This way, they could continue from the same point with the same people while going mobile. Additional value added services could also be attached to existing solutions. With location technology, people interested in similar issues could be able to chat according to their current position. Also, alert messages would bring additional excitement and unpredictability to the chatting. For example: "The Angel (alias) is within 500 meters of you. Would you like to send her a message?"

Some other location-based community services have different finders, where family members and friends are able to request each others' positions. Meetings could be arranged according to the location of a friend and elderly people could be tracked for their security. Naturally, these solutions can be integrated into other mobile applications like instant messaging and voice communication. Location-based community services have high revenue potential, because they are suited for instant mobile communication with small screen devices.

Communication-oriented mobile portal technology can be exported easily because the tools are naturally international. Technical platforms do not require further changes besides language translation. Consecutively, there is no need to create local content because most content is created by users. E-mail, instant messaging, chat and calendars are applications that provide a framework for customer interaction and usage. Therefore, communication-oriented mobile portals can be maintained with relatively smaller costs than vertical or horizontal portals. The number of partners is also smaller because special content, enhanced security or financial transactions are not required.

Communication-oriented portal services are suited for mobile operators because most of the revenue comes from increased air time. Additionally, mobile operators seldom have strong horizontal or vertical content experience so their core competencies do not support content generation or the personalization technologies required for efficient user interface. Since location technology is integrated into the mobile network, operators may, with some help from a systems integrator, generate additional revenue from location-based community services. Communication-oriented mobile portals will benefit from loyal customers because they return day after day for e-mail, calendar and chat services. Many of the users are very loyal because changing to another service would mean a different e-mail address and problems with their existing calendar. Communication-oriented portals may eventually end up being the cash cows of mobile operators.

However, vertical and horizontal portals are also looking for ways to increase customer loyalty and generate additional revenue. They are actively seeking partnerships where both parties benefit. Mobile operators are not strong in content creation and aggregation and are looking for partners to expand their services. In the future communication-oriented portals and content providers are likely to cooperate, forming multinational partnerships and alliances.

TABLE 6.5 ▦ Multinational partnerships

Feature	Implications	Development strategies
Applications are naturally personal	▪ No personalization technology needed	Concentrate on the user interface and the scalability of the service. Consider the opportunities for advertisers in the future.
Mass-market tools known from the internet	▪ Little customer education needed – faster adoption ▪ Economies of scale	Be the first in the market. This is the only way to lock the customers to your e-mail, your calendar and your value added services. Consider partnerships with horizontal portals.
Applications are location-independent	▪ Customers can read their e-mail and calendar anywhere ▪ Time sensitivity becomes important	Focus on real-time delivery of the messages. Categorize the messages according to importance and time sensitivity. This way, users could receive messages coming from certain addresses directly, without delays.
The platform can be exported	▪ Opportunity for software developers to export their products	Early movers are able to generate substantial profits from companies setting up communication-oriented portals. Acquire venture capital to be able to market internationally.
The service provider does not produce content	▪ Less partners ▪ Less maintenance ▪ Less fixed costs	Partner with horizontal and vertical portals in order to provide a wider array of services. Concentrate on scalability and marketing to reach a critical mass users.
Revenue from the increased air time	▪ Mobile operators are often the service providers ▪ Others have to agree on revenue sharing or establish a unique billing system	Partner with mobile operators to agree on revenue sharing. Develop premium services to increase the revenue. Consider business models with advertised content.

Mobile commerce-oriented

Mobile portals specializing in commerce develop payment and security solutions actively. This work is usually done in cooperation with device manufacturers, financial institutions and security solution providers. Also, different forums and industry consortiums participate in the process. Mobey

Forum, formed by Nokia, Ericsson and Motorola, together with financial institutions, is one of the consortiums driving the use of mobile devices in transactions. Additionally, some development work has been done by WAP Forum in terms of standardization. Radicchio, formed by Finnish operator Sonera and some partners, is aiming to create secure online payment solutions where operators would be the trusted third parties, offering authentication services for online transactions.

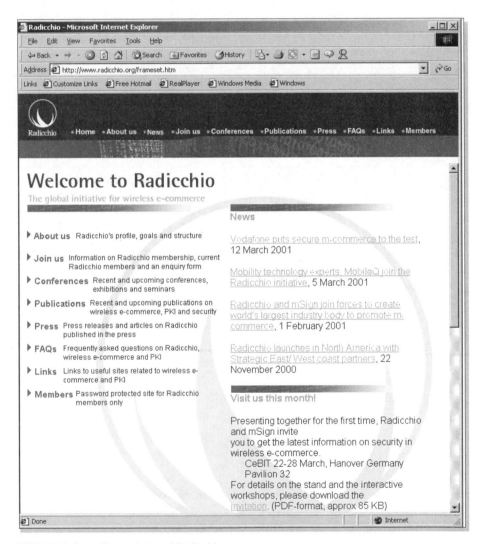

FIGURE 6.6 ■ The website of Radicchio

Banks and stock brokerages are natural players to offer mobile commerce services are because they already have the infrastructure and processes in place. Additionally, banks have strong brands and a reputation of being dependable and secure. The other reason for banks to move into the direction of mobile commerce is their concern about being disintermediated from the value chain. Other portal providers who focus on mobile commerce could apply for banking licenses to take the role banks fill today. Consumer behavior is moving away from cash towards electronic transactions and payment methods, so this is a real concern.

Commerce-oriented mobile portals aim to build scalable platforms and shopping carts for companies wanting to sell their products online. Therefore, they are just another way to get players together in order to achieve economies of scale and a critical mass of visitors. The merchants of the mobile portal pay a flat fee for an opportunity to sell their products via a mobile channel. In addition, they may pay a license fee according to the revenue. In return, the merchants have a shopping cart for their customers, secure payment processing and marketing efforts from the portal provider. A transportation company may offer logistics to all the merchants.

However, most products with great success potential are non-material. They can be purchased in an impulsive manner whenever the user needs them. With mobile commerce, time sensitive products that can be ordered regardless of the customer's location could be successful. In addition, workflow should be short and streamlined because the limited text input capabilities do not encourage the use of services with long forms to fill.

Some non-material products for commerce-oriented portals could be:

➤ hotel, taxi, restaurant reservations;
➤ (electronic) tickets for movies, concerts, exhibitions…;
➤ electronic maps and books;
➤ stocks;
➤ betting;
➤ gambling;
➤ auctions;
➤ music.

Additionally, mobile portals specializing in commerce could find ways to link existing services to location technology. For example, when a customer is ordering movie tickets, the default theater would be the one closest to her. The use of location technology would make it possible to create new services like location-based shopping, where the customer would see only the discounts of those stores close to him. This way, the physical world and mobile commerce is integrated and the personal features of the mobile device are used actively.

Almost all products and services well-suited for mobile commerce require complex, real-time software architectures in order to be efficient. All reservations, for example, need a real-time connection between the portal site and the providing company. What if there are no more tickets? How to choose a seat? Smoking or non-smoking? Which movie, which time? There are numerous reasons why online connection between the two systems is needed. Therefore, companies with up-to-date, real-time systems have a head start in the mobile commerce race.

There are also exceptions. In restaurants, the head waiter could receive reservations directly to his mobile terminal via an instant message and respond to them right away.

TABLE 6.6 ▪ Development of real-time software

Feature	Implications	Development strategies
Security and payment	▪ Companies develop solutions for secure payment ▪ Terminals are equipped with smart cards, such as Wireless Identification Module (WIM), that are capable of providing security	Participate in industry important consortiums and pilots. Develop partnerships with leading payment and security companies
Financial institutions offer commerce-oriented portals	▪ Banks move to mobile space in order to retain direct customer relationships ▪ Banks have a good reputation of being secure and dependable	Other mobile portal providers (horizontal, vertical …) should closely follow the situation and choose their strategy. They can either ▪ Partner with banks to offer offering products for security and payment ▪ Partner with operators offering products for security and payment ▪ Develop such an expertise in-house

Feature	Implications	Development strategies
The ordering process is time sensitive	■ External connections are used actively ■ Companies need real-time connection to their back-end systems. ■ Instant messaging is used	Develop the corporate systems in cooperation with systems integrators. Focus on netcentric, time sensitive solutions.
Non-material products	■ New ways for distribution ■ Time sensitivity is important	Examine the target audience and try to find out what products are best suited for mobile commerce. Do not try to sell everything online.
Companies strive to deliver more value to the customer	■ Location technology is used to offer new services	Follow the development of location-based services. Cooperate with technology providers and mobile operators.

Portal strategies for different players

Establishing a mobile portal requires a variety of skills and capabilities. All the players in the value chain have their own core competencies which they count on primarily when planning mobile ventures. Additionally, their position in the value chain has an effect on their success. Players without direct customer contact have to move into a position where it becomes possible to develop partnerships with companies that have it. On the other hand, companies with a direct customer interface may be in danger of losing it because of the market dynamics in mobile internet. If they fail to follow usage patterns and the development of the new technology, there is a chance that some players will be removed from the value chain by other members.

As mentioned before, no one player is able to produce every service by itself. Therefore, partnerships and joint ventures are inevitable and even recommended. Companies are looking for partnerships to reduce the time to market and acquire capabilities and knowledge they need for successful market entry. There are basically four types of partnerships needed in mobile portal development.

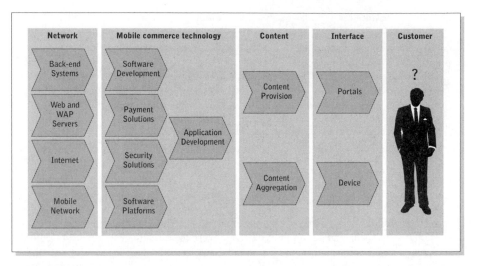

FIGURE 6.7 ■ The value chain of mobile commerce is complex and requires a number of different players. Companies are making strategic moves in order to acquire better control of the value chain. The portal is an ultimate goal for those players who want a direct customer relationship and strong visibility in consumer markets

They focus on:

➤ technology cooperation;

➤ synergy strategies, the building of critical mass and economies of scale;

➤ content cooperation, e.g. linking content to geographical coordinates;

➤ control strategies: getting better control of the value chain.

Almost all companies in the value chain need technology cooperation. Linking players together is an enormous task and systems integrators are in a key position to provide their services to everybody. The new services are time sensitive, location-aware and personal. The technology is complex and requires real-time connections among the producers. Some special attention is focused on instant messaging, management of metadata and database connectivity. It has been said that the only people who really made money during the gold rush were the people selling shovels. This may not be the case with mobile commerce, but it definitely is something to keep in mind. Mobile commerce success stories will be written by companies providing basic infrastructure and system integration to the various players in the value chain.

Companies establish partnerships with their competitors or other players in the value chain to acquire critical mass and economies of scale. Content providers join together to be able to compete against strong brands in the same field. Financial institutions and mobile operators cooperate to combine their customer base and provide horizontal portal services for everybody. Insurance companies and banks are looking for synergy when entering into mobile portal business. All of the cases above demonstrate synergy strategies that companies deploy in order to reach a win-win situation in mobile portal markets. This way, they are able to build critical mass and market the services faster because their customer base is extensive and well structured.

Content cooperation takes place for partly the same reasons. While content is one of the basic components of a successful portal, the companies are looking for ways to differentiate from competitors. Additionally, players without, or with little, content need to seek partnerships with companies that are able to deliver information services. Content cooperation also takes place because content providers need to find ways to link their information into geographical coordinates. Therefore, they partner with systems integrators and mobile operators to build a new generation of location-based services. Another reason for their cooperation is to get involved in their portal strategies. Also, banks are interesting partners for content providers because they do not have a wealth of information but they still want to establish mobile portals.

Control strategies are needed because some players are likely to be removed from the value chain if they cannot find a suitable partner. Mobile operators have an extremely strong position in the value chain of mobile portals. They control network usage, billing relationships and location information of the handsets. Therefore, some players are taking direct action to prevent themselves from being disintermediated.

Banks, for example, have basically three main strategies against operators offering financial services:

➤ cooperate with content providers and device manufacturers to establish a mobile portal (retain direct customer relationship);

➤ establish a mobile portal with a mobile operator (retain direct customer relationship);

➤ develop financial products (debt recovery, finance) for mobile operators offering financial services (lose direct customer relationship).

TABLE 6.7 ■ Strengths and weakness of value chain players

Player	Strengths	Weaknesses
Web portal	■ Internet business experience ■ Established partners ■ Wealth of content ■ Most of the infrastructure for the mobile channel is already in place (web servers, content management, connection to advertisers...)	■ Lack of knowledge of the mobile environment ■ No billing infrastructure ■ No access to location information of the mobile handsets ■ Lack of experience in mobile revenue models. Since advertising is not going to be the primary revenue source in the short term, web portals have to generate revenue from value added services or establish revenue sharing agreements with mobile operators
Content provider or aggregator	■ Wealth of content ■ Usually another channel for information (TV, radio, print media)	■ Small number of partners ■ No billing infrastructure ■ Lack of knowledge on mobile environment ■ No access to location information of the mobile handsets
Operator	■ Knowledge of mobile networks and development ■ Billing infrastructure ■ Direct customer relationship ■ Ability to locate consumers ■ Extensive customer base	■ Lack of internet experience ■ Culturally standards oriented and slow compared to internet companies ■ Little experience with data services
Financial institution	■ Strong brand ■ Security expertise ■ Payment expertise ■ Extensive customer base ■ Direct customer relationship	■ Lack of knowledge of the mobile environment ■ No access to location information of the mobile handsets ■ No content
System integrator	■ Experience with back-end systems ■ Ability to leverage the knowledge of large corporations ■ Knowledge of business models ■ Experience from several similar projects ■ Number of players in the value chain: system integrators are needed often along the value chain	■ Weak opportunities to establish own portal, therefore, system integrators specialize in providing support for the other players

Player	Strengths	Weaknesses
Application developer	■ Knowledge of business models ■ Knowledge of efficient applications for mobile customers ■ Experience from similar projects	■ Weak opportunities to establish own portal, therefore, application developers specialize in providing support for the other players
Device manufacturer	■ Strong knowledge of device features ■ Established partners ■ Knowledge of mobile networks ■ Ability to create custom features based on special handsets (security, payment...)	■ Competition from customers. Many portal providers are also the customers of device manufacturers. This is a controversial situation for a device manufacturer wanting to set up their own portal site

Web portals

Traditional internet portals have successfully integrated several applications into one value added service. They have partnered with several content and technology providers and a number of other companies to build online interfaces, integrating commerce, advertising and content into a lucrative package. Additionally, web portal providers have extensive experience with business models and successful strategies for the internet environment. Therefore, they are able to create customer "stickiness" and attractive community services while maintaining control in the changing markets. Traditional portal providers are also familiar with the dynamic market structure of internet business and they are able to leverage their knowledge across the organization.

Additionally, different organizations are connected to web portals using internet technology. With a net-centric architecture, partners are able to deliver their information with a real-time connection. Therefore, advertising and commerce is linked to third parties who provide usage monitoring, security and payment services.

Because of this background, traditional web portals are positioned well in terms of mobile portal services. Since the mobile portals are built on net-centric architecture, web portals have a head-start compared to the other companies. They already have internet know-how in their organization and people skilled to develop web services. A step further into mobile WAP services is not a leap into the unknown. Additionally, the same web servers can be used for mobile information provisioning because the only additional component in WAP architecture is the gateway between the web server and the internet.

However, traditional web portals have little knowledge of mobile networks and the future technologies needed in the mobile environment. Although they have strong experience with internet business models, the same concepts may not be viable in a mobile environment. Additionally, most internet portals do not have a billing relationship with their customers. Because revenue is based on advertising, they might not have any kind of database of the people visiting the site. Also, the mobile revenue models are strange to them because most of the money comes from increased air time and premium services. Advertising, as a revenue model, is likely to take off later on when mobile terminals develop and location-based services become widespread.

To develop the expertise needed in the mobile environment, traditional portals may take several different approach strategies:

- establish partnerships with a mobile operator, a handset manufacturer or a technology platform provider;
- develop expertise in-house with seminars and competency projects;
- acquire skilled personnel by recruitment.

Main strategies

Assuming that a traditional portal wants to explore the possibilities of the mobile environment and takes an approach to provide portal services, several strategic directions can be emphasized:

1. Focus on secure mobile commerce using a multichannel strategy. Provide secure payment options for mobile customers. This way, they are able to use the fixed internet for browsing the product catalog and a mobile terminal for buying time sensitive items. Customers are also able to personalize the service using a fixed internet interface so that their personal information does not have to inserted again when using a mobile channel. This strategy is possible in countries with high internet and mobile penetration.

2. Focus on mobile commerce in general. Develop location-based commerce solutions where customers are able to make impulse purchase decisions based on their location. Build a platform for online taxi, restaurant and ticket reservations. Make a mobile auction service.

3. Focus on mobile communication with a multichannel approach. Use the ubiquity and time sensitivity of mobile devices to integrate the existing services into a mobile environment. Send e-mail messages to mobile phones. Create communities that integrate web and mobile interfaces. Use instant messages to enable mobile chat services.

4. Focus on value added services. Create premium services with location and personalization technology. Send real-time financial news via instant messages to customers. Localize the search engine to provide location-based search results. Act as an intermediary, providing mobile yellow pages to consumers. Develop concepts where advertisers are able to use the mobile channel.

After deciding on the strategic approach, a traditional portal provider has to consider which possible partners will make the service viable.

Partner with a financial institution

Financial institutions and traditional portals might already have cooperation regarding online payments and financing. The new market situation, where financial institutions are in danger of being disintermediated by the mobile portals, might lead to a situation where banks would like to have stronger control of the mobile value chain. Therefore, traditional portals and banks are able to establish joint ventures in which both parties could benefit.

If a traditional portal decides to take a commerce-oriented approach to the mobile channel, banks are ideal partners. They are able to deliver secure payment mechanisms and leverage the extensive customer base into the mobile environment. Additionally, banks have strong brands which are usually associated with security, reliability and trustworthiness. Therefore, offering mobile payment and commerce solutions, together with a bank, might prove to be successful. However, portal providers should be careful not to exclude any customers if they are not the customers of the partnering bank. Everybody should be offered means to pay online.

Partner with a systems integrator

A communication-oriented mobile portal is a way to build customer relationships and loyalty. E-mail, especially, has good potential to become a killer application of the mobile environment because customers already know how to use it from the fixed internet. Additionally, substantial increases in service level can be achieved by providing location-independent, time sensitive messages which are sent directly to a mobile phone. This way, a person can be reached from anywhere and can access messages as soon as they hit the inbox. Real-time, anyplace e-mail will create a whole new communication atmosphere where important decisions can be made within minutes because all the parties involved can be reached within a short period of time.

Systems integrators are ideal partners for developing a communication-oriented mobile portal. They are able to leverage their knowledge from various projects and have experience with communication technologies. In addition, systems integrators are able to provide support later on, when new network technologies emerge. Traditional portals will need systems integrators in order to integrate existing and mobile applications together. Naturally, customers want to use the same e-mail address with both channels. Also, bulletin boards, vertical communities and discussion groups have some features that would bring additional value to users if they were available on mobile devices.

In most cases, there are several ways to agree on billing mechanisms. Some systems integrators may use a combined model, where part of the job is paid on an hourly basis and part of it is based on value-based billing. Value-based billing is used to share the risk of the venture by agreeing on certain indicators which determine the value of the work. Indicators for communication-oriented portals might be the number of users, revenue generated or increased number of users during a specified time.

Communication-oriented mobile portals require less maintenance than horizontal and commerce-oriented portals. This is because the amount of changing content is smaller. Customers are offered mobile e-mail and calendar applications and, therefore, they create the content by themselves. Naturally, when the service offering becomes wider and they are offered vertical communities and chat, the amount of maintenance increases. However, the partners do not have such an important role in communication-oriented portals as they do with horizontal.

Traditional portal providers typically own web servers and network infrastructure. This infrastructure can be used when offering mobile portal services with a communication-oriented approach. Depending on the existing solution, e-mail and news servers can be used with upgraded software. There are already plenty of packages offering out-of-the-box solutions for mobile e-mail, calendar and database connectivity. An additional WAP server is needed if the company wants to offer WAP-based communication solutions. With communication-oriented portals, the mobile operator functions as a facilitator. Obviously, the consumer needs to have a mobile operator who offers data services in order to contact the portal, but the only revenue the operator is getting is the value of the data transfer.

Partner with a mobile operator

The emergence of mobile data services will be characterized by joint ventures between mobile operators and traditional web portals. Mobile operators are looking for internet specialists capable of providing knowledge on business models, technology and usage patterns of the online population. They also need a partner to provide information about online culture and the market dynamics. Portal providers have established partnerships with several content providers who they use with mobile portal services as well, so web portals are interesting partners for mobile operators.

Why are web portals engaging in partnerships with mobile operators if they would be able to provide the service without them? One of the reasons is the superior distribution channels of mobile operators. They are able to modify the default settings of the phones and are, therefore, in a key position to control the distribution channels. Additionally, they have a direct billing relationship with the customer. This enables small payments to be paid along with the telephone bill. Therefore, the expensive and time consuming process of establishing billing infrastructure can be skipped. One payment channel is convenient from the customer's point of view as well. This way, she is able to see all the purchased items at a glance when the bill arrives. Customers are likely to be hesitant to establish multiple billing relationships with various portal providers, so mobile operators are interesting partners for Web portals.

Mobile operators are able to locate the handsets and transfer that information to third parties. Web portals have numerous services, in which the location of the user could bring substantial benefits for all the parties involved. The customers could use search engines, where all of the matches would be returned according to the location of their handsets. On the other hand, service providers could track user habits better and connect usage patterns to location information. Additionally, they would be able to develop advertising concepts, in which highly targeted ads are provided according to the keywords and locations of the user. This way, a customer searching for "hamburger" would see an ad for the closest fast food restaurant. In return for accepting the ads, the customer could receive free voice calls or some other services with a low margin. Location-based services are very hard to produce without partnerships with mobile operators. There are some other ways to locate the handset, but network-based location is likely to be the easiest and most convenient solution for consumers. The only exception is for car systems, in which a fixed GPS receiver is used. GPS uses satellites in order to determine the location of a car and, therefore, network-based location technologies are not used.

Yet another point drives mobile operators and web portals together: the mobile operator's knowledge of the emerging network technologies and their features. The combined expertise of web portal business models and mobile network characteristics provides the players with a solid foundation, equipped for success. This way, both parties are able to leverage their knowledge by sharing information and creating multichannel services, accessible via both mobile terminals and a fixed internet connection.

Develop expertise in-house and use existing content providers

Web portals can also choose to develop their core competencies systematically by building a mobile portal in-house. This way, they are able to experiment with the characteristics of the mobile environment and see which services users are likely to choose. However, it seems clear that the news and other generic information which is usually offered by web portals will become a commodity over time. Web portals should focus on value added services which produce differentiated content to mobile users. The services should focus on the key characteristics of mobile phones: time sensitivity, location independence and intimacy. Additionally, web portals have a great asset in their online, fixed internet services. They should take a multichannel approach, combining both interfaces together. The wealth of the content provided by existing content providers can be reused when developing mobile services. It is likely that the existing vertical communities can be extended to the mobile environment. PC-based chat and other community services can be developed to answer the needs of mobile users. This increases customer loyalty and "stickiness" because participants can use whatever channel is the most convenient.

One of the most critical issues in web-based portal service is the quality of content. The portals are tied to the content providers and vice versa. In a mobile environment, this relationship will be even more crucial. The content has to be time sensitive and personal because the users do not want to browse the mobile internet in the same way they use the fixed internet. The information they are looking for has to be available without delay or additional searching.

There are roughly two ways to produce mobile content for a portal site.

1. The web portal produces mobile services in-house from the "raw" content delivered by the content providers. In this case, personalization and instant messaging are controlled by the portal. This requires more resources and expertise, but helps the portal to acquire knowledge of the mobile environment and its special characteristics. In this model, the portal is able to change the content provider and compete with the different companies providing content.

2. The web portal outsources mobile services. This requires fewer resources and frees them up to be used elsewhere. However, the stability of the service has to be guaranteed by making revenue sharing agreements. If the content provider decides to work with someone else, the web portal is not able to continue the service. In addition, revenue sharing agreements secure the quality of the content and motivate the content provider to develop new, innovative concepts.

Web portals with customer billing relationships have a great advantage over others. They are able to provide value added content and premium services with a direct customer relationship. This way, they can also charge for the third parties that sell products and services online. Portals without billing relationships will have difficulties charging for content.

Basically, they have three revenue models:

- advertising;
- revenue sharing deals with a mobile operator based on increased air time;
- a cut of the revenues of the third party merchants.

Web portals that decide to develop a mobile portal alone are limited in the services they are able to offer. They do not have access to network-based location information; therefore, the development of location-based services becomes extremely difficult if not impossible. Obviously, the user can be asked to locate himself every time he uses a location-based service, but, in most cases, this is a clumsy and user-unfriendly concept. However, some less targeted (city-level) services could be possible with a user-determined position. Another limitation to going forward alone is the absence of payment methods offered by mobile commerce. Mobile payments would have to be processed directly, with the companies who are selling their products via a mobile channel.

The web portal that decides to tackle the mobile channel without partners also has other problems. It lacks an efficient marketing channel because the default settings are set by mobile operators and device manufacturers. Therefore, the best solution in their position is to deliver the mobile portal settings via fixed internet interface. The settings can be sent directly to a mobile terminal via instant messaging. This way, the only information the customer has to provide is the telephone number of the mobile phone. Another challenge is to compete against the other portals provided by mobile operators, content providers and, possibly, financial institutions. Customers will determine their choice from a wide variety of services. The ones offering the most valuable services with the lowest price and efficient distribution channels will be the winners.

▚ CASE STUDY

Rethinking the distribution channel

The distribution channel is one of the most important issues in determining the success of mobile portal services. While automatic setting configuration (mentioned above) using instant messaging requires action from the user, the default settings given by mobile operators and device manufacturers are already there without additional efforts. The situation is similar to web browsers that have default addresses to the portal sites of their interest. Both Microsoft Explorer and Netscape Navigator have default links to their own portal sites. Therefore, mobile operators and device manufacturers are in a key position to modify the default settings of mobile devices.

Yahoo! Europe and Siemens are cooperating to drive traffic into Yahoo! WAP sites. Siemens have committed to build direct access to WAP content provided by Yahoo! into upcoming WAP phones. Some of the services are Yahoo! Finance, Yahoo! Weather, Yahoo! Mail and Yahoo! Sports.

In North America, America Online and Motorola are developing a co-branded mobile device that provides access to AOL e-mail and AOL Instant Messager. AOL is also cooperating with Nokia to equip future terminals with default access to AOL services.

Content providers

Main strategies

Depending on size, brand and market situation, content providers have several possible approach strategies concerning mobile services.

The main strategies are:

- establish own portal service;
- establish a portal with selected partners;
- provide content for one mobile portal;
- provide content for multiple mobile portals.

However, these approaches are not mutually exclusive. A content provider may choose to establish its own portal while providing content for other players in the field. The big players in the content providing business, like Reuters, can take this approach because they have many resources and a very strong brand. Smaller companies, with less well-known brands, are likely to concentrate on providing content for established partners.

Develop an independent mobile portal

Strong content providers are establishing independent portals to attract more customers and build their brand among consumers. They focus on delivering the content directly to the customer without any intermediaries. This way, they acquire a direct customer relationship and are able to build target profiles according to usage patterns. In addition, content providers will rely on the increased revenue as mobile commerce and its services explode in the future. Therefore, the approach to building an independent portal is a strategic move to secure future revenues. The competition in the content business is becoming harder and companies are looking for ways to guarantee a direct channel to customers. Having a direct customer relationship assures that the content providers have at least one channel in the future if their position in the mobile value chain is endangered.

An independent mobile portal enables content providers to have direct control over both the business model and development issues. They are able to deploy the advertising concepts and mobile commerce capabilities that are best suited for their business model and company culture. Building one's own mobile portal is also a tactical approach to move up in the value chain. This way, a content provider is no longer just a subcontractor, delivering information to third parties. Becoming a horizontal portal enables content providers to influence customers and build their corporate brand in consumer markets.

Development of an independent mobile portal is costly because there are no partners to share the expenses. Special expertise is needed and development ties up a lot of resources that could otherwise be used for building the core competencies of content provision. The quality of mobile content is also important because it determines the target audience. Vertical content for special interest groups attracts a limited number of people, so, revenue has to come from targeted advertising and premium services. These customers may be more loyal and less expensive to reach than horizontal target groups. Basically, time sensitive content which may be personalized and utilized regardless of the customer's position has good potential to attract an audience. Financial news and schedules are examples of content that should attract customers. They are both time sensitive, mobile and can be personalized to answer the needs of an individual.

Content providers with limited capabilities should focus primarily on vertical communities that deliver substantial value to users. This way, they can market, experiment and develop the services with smaller costs than if they start with a horizontal, mass market approach. The infrastructure needed is less expensive and mistakes can be corrected faster, with less harm to the corporate brand. Vertical communities may be built faster and the company may already have the content needed for it. The time to market is short and development takes place in small cycles.

Content is always in danger of becoming a commodity. Numerous companies offer content for free to reach their own content-driven goals and expectations. Many internet companies offer free content to sell more online. Some benefit from advertising revenues. Therefore, content providers should watch the development of the mobile internet closely and try to find out if their niche markets are prepared to pay for information. How would you be able to link the content to location? What content is to be delivered to a mobile handset in real-time? How can sponsored content be delivered to a mobile terminal? These are some questions critical for mobile portal providers.

Customer loyalty is another big issue concerning content-driven portals. Are customers so excited about the content that they return to the site regularly? What happens to the portal if equivalent information is offered through other services? Content providers developing their own portal should consider offering communication-oriented portal services to increase customer loyalty. Mobile e-mail and calendar may not be within the core competencies of content providers, but they are able to secure at least a certain level of customer loyalty. This way, the portal provider would ensure that the customer returns to the site day after day.

CASE STUDY

Reuters

Reuters is moving into a mobile space by using various different distribution channels. It has established a mobile WAP site offering content to business professionals and consumers. In addition, Reuters is partnering with Vodafone AirTouch to provide real-time financial news through SMS messaging. The service costs approximately $15 per month and the subscriber gets new financial news on his mobile phone as soon as it hits the markets. SMS revenues are shared between Reuters and Vodafone AirTouch.

With these services, Reuters is moving up in the value chain in order to acquire a direct customer relationship instead of providing content for third parties exclusively. It aims to strengthen the brand image in the eyes of consumers while generating additional revenue from partnerships with operators.

Joint venture with a mobile operator

As noted before, mobile operators have a strong position in the value chain of mobile commerce. They have network expertise and knowledge of mobile service delivery. They also control the distribution channel, location-based services and customer interface in terms of billing. However, they have little experience with content or internet services in general. Therefore, content providers would be suitable partners for operators. In partnerships, mobile operators would probably be the dominant player because, simply, the business case favors them. However, a content provider could use the operator's billing infrastructure for charging premium services. Additionally, content-driven mobile commerce becomes possible.

The mobile operator can use another channel of the content provider (TV, Radio or print) to advertise services and create multichannel concepts for mobile commerce. Newspapers for example, can be used to market the products and services of the mobile channel. Limitations in screen size and text input can be overcome by deploying a multichannel approach where the customer can conveniently read most of the information from the newspaper and order the product using his mobile phone.

Provide content for other portal sites

The quality of content has to be very high because mobile customers cannot tolerate low usability and information that is not relevant to them. Personalized, location-sensitive and time-sensitive content is going to be an absolute necessity for mobile portals. The importance of context also becomes important. Portal sites will expect to have content that meets the expectations of customers.

There are two strategic directions for content providers:

➤ content provision for one portal;

➤ content provision for multiple portals.

If content providers choose the first option, agreements have to be based on long term goals and revenue sharing because they are relying on a single source of revenue. The risk of disintermediation or failure is high and the company should develop risk management scenarios. The best way to guarantee a position in the value chain of the future is to develop highly specialized content products for partners. This way, the portal site could not deliver the same service level without the content provider. When delivering content for a single portal, the content provider should move in the value chain and start to develop applications and solutions for mobile information provisioning. By moving in the direction of application development, the content provider could introduce differentiated products to the market, enabling time sensitive and location-dependent information delivery.

Content provisioning for multiple partners is less risky. If one of the ventures fails and cannot pay for content any more, there are always other customers left. This way the risk is shared and operations can reach economies of scale. The same information, more or less, is delivered to all customers via a real-time internet connection. Although this model enables content providers to develop their core competency, it has a risk of disintermediation as well. Customers are able to purchase "raw" content from content providers because they develop the applications needed for personalization and location. This way, content providers face increasing competition over time because they are actually delivering raw material for processing. Therefore they should differentiate from their competitors by developing concepts and applications specifically for the mobile environment.

▦ CASE STUDY

Oracle

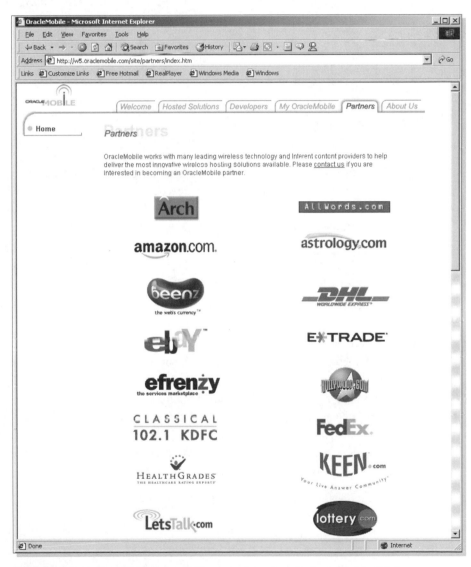

FIGURE 6.8 ▩ OracleMobile.com offers a variety of content provided by third party developers

In February 2000, Oracle established a wireless portal service, OracleMobile.com, that bundles content from various sources and companies. Some content providers are Amazon.com, eBay, Lottery.com, Travelocity.com, Waiter.com, MapQuest and the Weather Channel. OracleMobile.com is based on Oracle's portal platform called Portal-To-Go and it includes features such as quick alerts, service pre-sets and location-based services.

Mobile operators

Main strategies

Mobile operators cannot miss the emerging opportunities of mobile commerce. The margin from voice traffic is decreasing and the competition over basic network services becomes harder over time. Investments in third generation networks are massive and they have to find ways to cover the costs and justify the expenses. Mobile data services are expected to become reality as the customers want to have access to their e-mail, calendar and corporate data using mobile terminals. Additionally, it has been noticed that even the voice revenue increases as the customers begin to use mobile data services.

Fixed internet portals are built in order to increase customer loyalty and satisfaction by providing all services within a single environment. Also, mobile customers are following the same pattern. Therefore, mobile operators want to offer portal services which increase the air time and generate extra revenue from premium services. However, there is a substantial cultural difference between the internet and the telecom world. internet companies are used to fast development cycles, market-driven development and innovative collaboration. In contrast, telecom companies have traditionally had slower, engineering-driven cultures, where standards and hardware are in a dominant position. Therefore, the cooperation between the two worlds is not an obvious success.

There are four main strategies for mobile operators:

➤ develop own portal;

➤ license a portal from software developers;

➤ form strategic partnerships to provide portal services;

➤ act as a facilitator, concentrate on your core competency.

The last option may be the right one for those operators with limited resources. Even without their own portal, operators have a strong market situation because they are able to offer payment services for portal providers in their network. Additionally, they have control over the location technology in their network, enabling next generation data services based on the position of the user. Mobile operators also have an extensive customer database that can be used for target marketing.

Develop own mobile portal

Mobile operators with extensive resources and skilled people can develop their own portal. This requires internet expertise and, therefore, the operators with fixed-internet portals have a head-start over those without any internet experience. However, the development of a mobile portal involves numerous tasks and, therefore, deployment requires assistance from software developers and systems integrators.

As a reminder, these are some of the components typically needed when establishing a mobile portal:

> content management;

> user management;

> security solutions;

> payment solutions;

> personalization technologies;

> web servers;

> database servers;

> application servers;

> WAP servers;

> marketing.

Additionally, connections to several companies are needed to import content and enable secure payment gateways to banks.

There are several options for operators to choose from when developing the portal platform. Some software development companies offer out-of-the-box portal platforms and commerce solutions for faster time to market. Additionally, Openwave, the provider of WAP gateways, integrates its portal platform into WAP gateways and other products. This way, operators do not have to build the platform from the beginning and development time can be cut down.

Basically, there are three options for a mobile operator:

➤ develop own portal;

➤ form strategic partnerships to provide portal services;

➤ license a portal from software developers.

The development of one's own portal is the most expensive and time consuming option. Some systems integrators can be used for integrating existing systems into a mobile environment but most of the job is done in-house. This approach is viable for companies that want to have something unique and different because there are already plenty of out-of-the-box platforms available. The possibility to sell the portal to other players in the industry and the ability to create services and concepts that do not exist with the available solutions are some of the reasons to start one's own portal development. Nordic companies, like Sonera (Finland) and Telia (Sweden), have both developed portal concepts that they sell all over the world. Sonera's Zed and Telia's MyDOF are mobile portal products. Both Telia and Sonera have small domestic markets where mobile phone penetration is reaching the saturation point. Therefore, these companies aim to go international in order to generate revenue from software sales.

Most mobile operators decide to build a portal in cooperation with selected partners. Systems integrators and application developers work in collaboration with operators in order to create successful services. Billing can be based on piece wages or revenue sharing agreements, ensuring the best effort from both sides. The partners also provide the content and communication technology needed for mobile e-mail and community services. The concept of having multiple partnerships providing services under one portal platform requires technical solutions, in which new partners can be attached to the service easily. Therefore, the platform has to be flexible to decrease the time to market for new applications. Seamless cooperation with a systems integrator is recommended. This way, new applications can be introduced faster because the systems integrator already knows the architectural requirements for integrating the two systems.

Licensing a portal might prove to be the fastest way to the markets. Players developing their own portals in small countries, like Sweden and Finland, are willing to sell their products internationally. Licensing a portal that has been tested in real markets is an ideal way for those operators with limited resources to go online. Some players enable operators to brand the licensed portal and, therefore, customers cannot tell the difference between a licensed and a developed portal.

Mobile operators who take the approach to develop their own mobile portal should consider their core competencies and aim to provide services that are best suited for them. With most operators, communication-oriented mobile portals are an ideal option because they do not require extensive, time sensitive content to be provided continually. In addition, communication-oriented portals have a high customer loyalty because users return to the site regularly. This increases air time and results in higher income from the services. Because communication-oriented portals aim to provide customers with the basic applications for communication, it does not require the same maintenance effort that the other portal types do. Additionally, the provision of a technical platform has always been one of the strengths of mobile operators because their business culture is typically more engineering-driven. Communication-oriented portals can be offered to a horizontal audience because almost everybody has some experience with e-mail from the fixed internet.

Communication-oriented portals can be extended later on to cover other horizontal services like news and mobile commerce. Mobile operators have an exceptional position in the value chain for offering a wide array of services because they control the billing relationship and location information. Therefore, operators should develop services all the time and focus on mobile commerce in which the telephone bill is used as a payment mechanism. Additionally, location-based services have great potential and operators should find ways to deliver the position coordinates of a handset to third parties who are developing those services. Security and revenue sharing are some issues for special consideration.

Join forces with a financial institution

Operators specializing in mobile commerce should consider cooperation with banks and other financial institutions. Some operators are already considering mergers with banks because they would like to offer financial services through their networks. It is likely that countries with high mobile phone penetration will have an extensive number of online banking customers. Therefore, mobile operators aim to get a share of this promising new market. Additionally, the revenue in mobile commerce is not expected to be in the provision of a network, but in the provision of financial services and payment models.

Financial institutions are good at secure payment services and their brand is often associated to security and reliability. Additionally they have a wide customer database with updated information about the usage patterns and behavior. Unlike many fixed internet portals, financial institutions have a direct relationship with their customers. This makes joint marketing viable, because the two customer bases can be combined together.

Joint venture with a financial institution should, naturally, focus on developing mobile commerce-oriented portals. Customers could have account and financing options when buying or selling through the portal service. Also, additional payment models for "bricks and mortar" businesses could be developed. Sonera, for example, has developed a concept of "Mobile Pay", which allows vending and car wash machines to accept payments via a mobile channel. The customer calls a certain number while close to the vending machine and the price is charged to his telephone bill.

Partner with a content provider or fixed internet portal

Mobile operators who partner with content providers and fixed internet portals should focus on the quality of content provided by the partners. The mobile environment is different from the fixed internet and, therefore, not all of the content is suitable for mobile portals. Concepts that combine time sensitivity, personalization and location-based services are going to be killer applications in the mobile era. Therefore, "raw" content should be processed to fit better into mobile terminals.

Cooperation between a fixed internet portal and a mobile operator usually leads to the provision of horizontal portal services that attract as many customers as possible. Therefore, customer loyalty and satisfaction may decrease as the provided applications and information are impersonal and generic. This may also cause problems with advertising and mobile commerce later on, because customer profiles are not known.

There are three ways to overcome the impersonal nature of horizontal portals:

1. Deploy personalization technology. Encourage customers to create their own profile for more personalized services and information.

2. Create vertical communities. By developing interest groups and social communities, customers can find the content they are looking for more easily. Later on, this also helps target advertising and innovate new commerce concepts.

3. Offer communication-oriented portal services. E-mail and chat communities are naturally personal. They also increase customer loyalty.

As the mobile internet develops, terminals are going to be more flexible and allow better navigation because screens and character input will improve. This will lead to situations where TV and radio advertisers invite mobile customers to visit their site to get more information about products. If mobile operators do not allow free browsing and take a "walled garden" approach to the mobile internet, customer satisfaction will most likely decrease. This way, the customers can only visit the sites offered by the mobile operator. Can you imagine a fixed ISP offering an internet connection, but only to their own site? They would be out of business very soon. Mobile operators have to consider opening their networks to everybody. The payment model has to be reconsidered. However, that is a less expensive option than losing existing customers. Additionally, television and radio advertisers could easily provide a service in which new customers send an instant message to a certain number and in return, receive connection settings directly to their mobile terminal. This model would lead to a situation in which customer flows avoid the mobile portal of the operator and head to other sites instead.

Financial institutions

Banks have traditionally focused on providing payment and financing services for their customers. As trusted third parties, they act as facilitators in commercial transactions, providing partners for debt recovery and authentication services. Additionally, banks have entered into electronic commerce by providing electronic banking and payment services that are usable with a standard web browser. The primary reason for banks to enter into the e-commerce world is the substantial decrease in electronic transaction costs. For banks, it is not the same if customers pay their bills facing a bank employee or facing a computer monitor. The transaction costs can be dramatically cut down when the majority of customers use electronic channels to handle their everyday banking routines.

In general, banks have a very strong position in electronic commerce. They are able to use their strong brand to increase customer confidence in commercial transactions. In addition, online customers can be offered direct payment methods in which the bank acts as a trusted third party. For example, in

Finland, 1.5 million banking customers (the whole population is 5 million) use the internet to pay their bills, check their account balance and transfer money to other accounts. The high internet and electronic banking penetration enables online stores to offer payment methods, in which customers can pay for purchased items directly through their internet bank account. This way, both parties involved in online commerce can be sure that they really are who they claim to be.

Because of the success in electronic commerce, many banks are looking into mobile channels to increase their online customer base. Within a couple of years, it is expected that there will be over a billion mobile phones on the market and most of the phones will offer secure banking and other financial services. Mobile phones are cheaper and more convenient to use than PCs. Therefore, they have enormous potential to serve banking customers from all walks of life. On the other hand, mobile devices are always small, equipped with limited screen and text input capabilities. The concept of fixed internet banking cannot be brought directly into the mobile environment.

Main strategies

Financial institutions have to follow the development of the mobile internet carefully to decide what strategic actions they should take in order to achieve a competitive edge over competitors within and outside the industry. Financial service providers have several directions to take because established structures have not yet taken place. Therefore, cooperation with some players in the field is recommended to acquire knowledge and benefit from similar goals.

In terms of partnerships, financial institutions should aim to deploy the following models:

1.   Synergy strategies. Cooperate with companies that have similar objectives and views of tomorrow. Bring your core competence skills to the table and encourage partners to deliver their expertise. This way, both participants are able to benefit from the synergy and learn from one another. For example, mobile operators and financial institutions are able to combine their customer bases together in order to market services in joint ventures.

2.   Control strategies. Develop concepts and procedures to ensure your position in the value chain of mobile commerce. Financial institutions should develop payment and security solutions in cooperation with

device manufacturers to be able to provide services in the future. Also, cooperation with mobile operators is recommended because, this way, they ensure that their payment solutions are used in the mobile marketplaces provided by the operators.

3. Technology cooperation. Cooperate with systems integrators, software developers and platform providers to develop the skills and knowledge needed in mobile commerce. Technology cooperation also takes place in the models above as the players in the financial industry develop technology solutions in cooperation. Also, joint ventures with device manufacturers aim to develop technical solutions.

Regarding mobile portal development, financial institutions have four main strategies to choose from:

1. Acquire more knowledge of mobile banking solutions and wait until customers are more receptive to electronic banking.

2. Follow the development closely and provide mobile banking services to customers. No active participation in portal development.

3. Provide mobile payment and financing to all portals. The services are portal-driven, focusing on solving some of the challenges regarding payment and security.

4. Develop your own portal. Innovate concepts and service models to increase customer loyalty and satisfaction. Establish a secure market place for third party merchants to generate additional revenue from transactions. Provide everything it takes to build a competitive and successful mobile portal, loaded with communication tools, news and entertainment.

The first option is relevant to those financial service providers who operate in markets with low mobile phone penetration and slow internet adoption. In these markets, customers are not used to handling their banking routines via electronic channels. Therefore, massive investment would be waste of money since the customers have no terminals on which to use the services.

The second option, providing mobile banking services to customers is viable in markets with emerging mobile phone penetration. In these countries, mobile portals are still weak and consumers are using mobile phones exclusively for voice communication. However, there is a trend towards higher mobile phone penetration and data-capable devices. Financial service providers should follow the development closely and educate customers to use electronic channels for banking routines. Therefore, the deployment of mobile banking or fixed internet banking is viable. In countries with high internet penetration financial service providers should consider establishing a multi-channel approach in which some services are offered through the fixed internet interface and some via a mobile channel. Naturally, services suited for mobile devices are fast and do not require a lot of text writing because the limited form factor of a mobile phone does not encourage the use of complicated processes.

Provide services for other portals

Mobile portal providers are likely to introduce market places and other commerce solutions sooner or later. As noted in Chapter 3, we have seen that the same patterns in the fixed internet do not apply in mobile commerce. Therefore, products and services sold over mobile networks will follow completely different business models and processes which require differentiation from the financial service provider's point of view. What kind of services are you able to provide for players that combine fixed internet, TV and radio? How about location-based services? What is the revenue model and how should the services be charged? Will you be able to innovate convenient ways to charge for micro-payments in premium content services? What kind of payment solutions can you develop for offline use of mobile phones using Bluetooth technology? As you can clearly see, there are numerous opportunities for innovative financial service providers who want to generate additional revenue from the new wave of mobile commerce.

For simplification from the financial service provider's point of view, mobile consumer transactions can be divided into three separate categories:

➤ consumer-portal provider transactions;

➤ consumer-merchant transactions;

➤ consumer-consumer transactions.

Consumer-portal provider transactions fall in to a category in which the mobile operator who has a direct billing relationship with the consumer has control of the customer relationship. Under this model, portal providers may offer payment services for third party merchants selling products in their mobile portal. The customer pays for the merchandise together with a monthly bill (telephone/premium service bill), and a cut of the revenue goes directly to the portal provider. This way the customer doesn't have to pay for the product immediately. The financial organization is passed over in terms of brand visibility and customer relationship. However, financial service providers are able to offer their services directly to the portal providers. Portal providers are reluctant to take on the risk of bad debt, especially for third parties. Financial organizations are able to provide financing and debt recovery services to portal providers deploying this transaction model.

Consumer-merchant transactions are direct payments between the buyer and the seller. The portal provider doesn't have to take the risk of bad debt because he is not involved in the transaction. On the other hand, the portal provider may still take his share from the revenue and charge an additional base fee to the merchants. Using this consumer – merchant transaction model, the portal provider has less risk but charging for micro-payments may be harder because it would be foolish to transfer three cents every time the customer uses a certain premium service. Therefore, a separate account for micro-payments has to be established between the information provider and the merchant. Usually, a customer transfers a certain amount of money to his private account and the account is debited every time he uses the service. Naturally, a bank transfer is needed to transport the money to the user's account. Banks should consider offering similar services to merchants, enabling small payments without the transfer. This way, the same account could be used regardless of the premium service and the banks would generate additional revenue by acting as an intermediary between the seller and the buyer.

Consumer – merchant transactions are also needed for the purchase of more expensive items. They can be paid using a bank transfer or credit card service provided by the sellers. To conduct online bank transfers, the customer has to have a bank that offers such services. With a password and an ID, the customer can access his bank account and commit the transfer. On the other hand, credit card number, name and the year of expiration is required for credit card transactions. Credit card companies are also developing concepts in which a smart card inside the phone could be used as an equivalent to a credit card. This way, the user simply pays for the items by entering his personal PIN code when it is required.

Financial organizations are passed over if the consumer–merchant transaction is conducted using cash. In some countries, products can be paid for when they are delivered or picked up from the post. This method is likely to be used if the security of online transactions cannot be guaranteed.

Consumer–consumer transactions are used in mobile commerce where auctions and similar actions take place. The portal provides the basic infrastructure where consumers are able to sell their merchandise directly to others. Consumer–consumer transactions are usually conducted using a bank transfer, cash or money order. With the emergence of mobile commerce, some other concepts have also been established. A Silicon Valley start-up, Pay-Pal, has developed an interesting way to transfer money in consumer–consumer transactions. To use the service, the user has to register his or her credit card information on the web page of Confinity. After that, the user may download software that is used as a purse. The users of Pay-Pal can transfer money between Palm Pilot devices using an infrared connection. As soon as the devices that are used for the money transfer go online, the money is transferred from one account to another. This type of service has many other purposes as well. In the future, something similar will be used to buy products from vending machines using Bluetooth as means of money transportation. Financial organizations are in a key position to develop these concepts.

Develop one's own portal

Financial institutions in developed mobile markets may consider setting up their own portal in order to ensure a direct customer relationship. Primarily, financial players are competing against the portals of mobile operators who have superior distribution channels and a direct billing relationship with the customer. With a mobile portal, a financial institution can increase customer loyalty and differentiate from competitors by providing value added services to customers. Additionally, some customers may regard a mobile interface as so important that they select their banks and stock brokerages according to the online services they offer. In this case, the financial operator could reach new customers by providing mobile services.

Developing one's own portal is not an easy way out. Numerous skills besides the core capabilities of financial institutions are required and, therefore, partnerships are highly recommended. Systems integrators, application developers and content providers are needed to build a portal platform capable of competing with the other services on the market. Additionally, the question of whether to subsidize the handsets or not should be answered. Obviously, handsets capable of internet banking will increase usage and generate more visitors to the portal. Whether this is enough to justify subsidization of the handsets is dependent on the markets and the current situation. Some reasons to do so might be:

➤ increased revenue from third party merchants selling their products via the portal;

➤ cost savings caused by increased online usage and decreased face-to-face transactions;

➤ new customers.

The services of financial institutions are competing against horizontal, vertical and communication-oriented portals. To lock customers into the service in a positive way, financial institutions should consider expanding their services in a direction in which customer loyalty can be strengthened. Introducing communication-oriented services could increase customer loyalty and cause regular visitors to the site. This way, mobile commerce services can also benefit from the regularity and wealth of customers.

Systems integrators and application developers

Systems integrators and application developers provide the other players in the value chain with back-end systems and custom applications capable of delivering the information into a mobile channel. Their core competence is technical knowledge about the requirements and software architecture needed in order to build mobile services. Systems integrators have expertise about back-end systems and application programming interfaces which are needed for building custom applications for the mobile environment. They are able to retrieve information from customer relationship management software, enterprise resource planning packages and various other legacy systems. This way, information can be used effectively and customers can be offered new, innovative services. For example, customer relationship management software can be used to create profiles for mobile users. According to the profiles, targeted precision advertising can be deployed to support some services. The customer can personalize the advertising messages and express his interests to the portal provider. In return, the customer may be given free voice calls or access to premium data services.

Also, location-based services require updated and modern legacy systems capable of data mining. Location-dependent search engines that provide information according to the position of the user require a database with geocoded information. When the user executes a search, the location coordinates of the user are submitted to the system, together with the keywords. After that, data mining takes place to match the keywords and location coordinates to the information in the database. In return, the search engine lists all the matches from a certain geographical area. When searching a keyword "museum" with a search criteria "10 kilometers", the system would return hyperlinks listing information about the museums within a radius of ten kilometers. Application developers and systems integrators are needed to set up the system, teach how to update the information and create custom applications that allow information to be transferred to a mobile terminal.

All the other players in the mobile commerce value chain should consider beginning to update legacy systems as soon as possible because, without efficient data mining and information delivery, modern mobile applications cannot be built. In addition, the development of real-time, net-centric legacy systems takes time and projects may delay the launch of mobile applications. Therefore, strategic decisions and directions regarding mobile services should be taken as soon as possible to ensure the development of efficient back-end systems. When legacy systems are updated, new mobile applications can be introduced faster and the time to market is cut down.

Main strategies

Systems integrators and application developers will make money in the beginning of the mobile commerce evolution. Portal providers have to update their databases and other systems to offer services that are suited to a mobile environment. Being time sensitive, personal and location-aware, the new services require custom applications and a scalable network architecture. Therefore, systems integrators and application developers should take a strategic approach now, to be prepared to answer the growing needs.

Some possible directions to take are the following:

1. Develop products for mobile commerce and information delivery. Use your core competencies, develop expertise in mobile environment and package the two into a special offer for portal providers.

2. Partner with companies offering products for mobile channels. Engage in partnerships with WAP server manufacturers, mobile operating system developers and portal platform providers in order to develop expertise and become a Value Added Reseller (VAR) of their products.

3. Specialize in a certain technology or business model suitable for the mobile internet environment. Fields with great potential are:

- personalization;
- data mining;
- payment;
- security;
- Bluetooth;
- instant messaging;
- location technologies;
- unified messaging;
- PIM (personal information management).

In addition, both application developers and systems integrators have to decide on the target audience. Depending on the market situation and current core capabilities, they can focus on business-to-business solutions or consumer markets. Companies focusing on corporate solutions should have deep knowledge of the corporate legacy systems and their integration. Corporate portals are complex and require integration of several back-end systems. The work is usually continuous and ensures long term relationships with stable revenue. On the other hand, consumer-oriented mobile portals may be built from scratch. Systems integrators and application developers have an opportunity to design the software architecture and network infrastructure from the beginning. Obviously, some systems integration may be needed to connect an existing customer database into the new platform but, compared to a corporate portal, the workload is smaller. The revenue model of consumer applications is likely to be different from corporate projects. Some application developers charge according to revenue generated by the application. This enables risk sharing and requires a closer partnership with the customer. This way, application developers, confident with their solutions, have an opportunity to generate substantial profit.

Develop market-driven applications

Application developers and systems integrators should pay special attention to the business requirements of the applications because they are technology-oriented companies. They should also acquire more knowledge of usability issues, revenue models and target audience to be able to generate more value to service providers. Expertise in technology is a necessity in application development but it should be used primarily for reaching business goals and expectations, not for it's own sake.

Not all applications can be transported into a mobile environment. A lot of services that are already available cannot compete with the other media in terms of usability and convenience. For example, would I read the political news from a tiny, screen and even pay for it? Never. Will I buy a T-shirt using my mobile phone? I doubt it. How about groceries? Do they have the potential to become killer items for mobile commerce? Unfortunately, the answer is no. Mobility itself is a nice thing that enables incredible service concepts and huge revenue opportunities. At the same time, the limitations of mobile terminals have to be taken into consideration. Mobile application developers should remember that there are many other means for providing information and shopping experience to consumers. A mobile channel is not likely to replace other media for services in which time sensitivity, mobility and personalization are not important.

Notes and references

1. "Wireless Portal Revenue To Skyrocket," allNetDevices, www.allnetdevices.com (June 26, 2000)

Index